Tell Me More about the Mark Degree

Tell Me More about the Mark Degree

Revd Neville Barker Cryer

First published 2007

ISBN (10) 0 85318 266 3
ISBN (13) 978 0 85318 266 5

Published by Lewis Masonic

an imprint of Ian Allan Publishing Ltd,
Hersham, Surrey KT12 4RG.
Printed in England by Ian Allan Printing Ltd,
Hersham, Surrey KT12 4RG

Typeset by FiSH Books, Enfield, Middx

Contents

Introduction

Following the publication last year of the 150th anniversary book for the Grand Lodge, *Marking Well*, it would be a quite proper question to ask why there is any need for something else so soon dealing with this degree. The answer is that the contents of this book were written long before the 150th celebrations were thought of and had been circulated among friendly Mark Masons, or delivered in Mark lodges as invitation lectures and demonstrations. As time has passed there have been requests for this private material to be made public and the publishers also have considered that there might be a wider audience to be served.

It is also the case that whilst the contents of last year's book dealt admirably with places and persons connected with the great event that it commemorated, this book is trying to serve the lodges and their members in the days ahead. At a time when there seems to be a growing, and commendable, desire to understand our Masonry as well as practise it, what is put down here has just that purpose in view. Each of the Ten Minute Talks that come first in this book are meant to help Mark Masons to appreciate and understand better the contents of our ritual and procedures. That they have already helped a few leads me to believe that others could benefit. What is undoubted is that I have myself, over the last 50 years, benefited from, and grown to value the lessons that Mark Masonry has to offer.

Should there be occasions when time for a lecture is available then perhaps the three offered here will avoid the necessity of always looking for an outside speaker. Certainly experience with my other books on the Craft and Royal Arch is such as to suggest that what has been written can be of help in lodges and chapters. Apart from any copyright on formal reproduction for gain there is free permission to reproduce in speech what is here, with due acknowledgement. It will please this author to know that he is assisting that famous 'daily advancement in Masonic knowledge'.

As for the old rituals that are reproduced here it may be of interest for readers to learn that not only have these been already translated into, and performed, in Dutch but that the author was invited as a special guest to see their presentation there three years ago. As is stated in their introduction they have for long been known to Surrey Freemasons and their neighbours. I shall be delighted to learn of their further use.

In commending this work to my present readership, and especially to those who share my long regard for Mark Masonry, I can only hope that once again there will be those who, on reading or hearing what is in these pages, will be led to exclaim, as others have done elsewhere: 'Well, I just didn't know that.' If that happens then all the effort of creation and publication will have been immensely worthwhile.

The Revd Neville Barker Cryer, M.A., PPGM (Surrey)
York. 2007

Ten 10 Minute Talks:

1. Mark Man and Mark Master

When the members of a Mark lodge have been assured that their candidate for the Mark Degree has attained the status of a Master Mason in the Craft, and prayer has been offered for the blessing of the occasion, a newcomer to the Mark is made aware of something that has happened from very much earlier times. He is told that it was then the custom for a fellow of the craft of stonemasons to be invited to choose a Mark that was special to himself, and unlike anything used by anyone else in that lodge, so that his work might be recognised as his by the officials called Overseers. He is also taught how to present that mark at the Senior Warden's wicket in the West that he might receive the wages due to him as a Mark Man. If he says that he had not received such a mark in his Craft lodge, as he still might do in many Scottish Craft lodges, he is taken to the Registrar's place which is beside the Secretary, and is provided with his distinctive mark. This is then presented to the Worshipful Master for confirmation. Because we so often pass over this part of the ceremony too swiftly at the outset of the present Mark degree ceremony we may easily forget that the candidate is then addressed by the Worshipful Master in the following manner: 'I admire the ability displayed in the execution of your work. I therefore designate you a Mark Man and will at once entrust you with the token of that rank.' He is accordingly shown how to present his hand for such wages as will thus be his due. Let us register here the fact that what has just taken place has confirmed our candidate in a new Masonic rank, that of Mark Man, even if he were not to proceed any further.

At once, however, in our present practice, he is said to be qualified for advancement to the honourable degree of a Mark Master. One might therefore reasonably ask why, if this is the real purpose of the evening's ceremony, is a distinction made between two ranks or grades in what is regarded as a one degree event. Why do we have two such steps and what do they each signify?

The answer, of course, is that what we have here is the remnant of what was, during a century before our present Mark Grand Lodge organisation was established. Let me explain. A working stonemason received his personal mark when he had qualified as a fellow or master craftsman, but not a master mason, of his trade. The master mason was then a person of a superior rank who did not even belong to the working lodge. So when a form of Mark practice began to be adopted by Free and Accepted Masons, used among them since at least 1750, it was that older usage which was followed. Fellowcrafts finished the second degree by being given a mark which thus allowed them to be paid their wages in specie in the middle chamber, as we are told was the case in the explanation of the second degree tracing board. These brethren were known as 'marked' or Mark men. That is why, to this day, when a Craft lodge is closed in what was originally the only form of ancient closing, in the fellows grade, the Senior Warden says, 'having seen that every Brother has had his due'. The apprentices did not have wages. It was only the fellow-craftsmen who were so entitled.

Yet there were some other kinds of mark that were used by working masons, as is explained in another of these talks. One was not granted until a man was qualified as a Harod or senior, thus able to preside as a ruler of an operative lodge. In the Free and Accepted Craft this further knowledge was not granted until a brother was raised to the so-called rank of a Master Mason, when you could become a Mark Master Mason. That is why, when the candidate today has received his mark the Worshipful Master says: 'that he may be qualified to preside over a lodge of Operative Masons when required'. In the 18th century there were indeed two separate and complete ceremonies which followed the second and third degrees respectively. A reconstruction of those two early ceremonies, taken from the original documents, can be found later in this book.

Today we have reduced those ceremonies to just one but by retaining the titles of Mark Man and Mark Master we have at least maintained the ancient practice and ensured that the present Mark Mason has taken both the essential steps. It only goes to prove that there is much more to our progress through Masonry than at first we may be aware of.

2. The use of the Mark

Mark Master Masons today could well be forgiven for thinking that the really important feature in this degree (or, rather, degrees) that they have taken, is the keystone. At the outset of our Mark traditions this was not the case. The important feature then was the granting and receiving of a personally chosen emblem as a mark, bearing in mind, however, that sons and heirs of a stonemason would be likely to adopt the same mark as their father or benefactor. As is made clear in another lecture in this book the practice of acquiring a mark forms the core of the first of the Mark degrees which was called that of Mark Man or Mark Mason. This is clearly expressed in the familiar words: 'In former times it was the custom in every Fellowcraft lodge for each fellowcraft to choose a mark by which his work might be known to his Overseer...'

That this was in fact the case is confirmed for us by some still extant evidence in Scotland. We have, in the library of one of the oldest lodges there, at Aberdeen, a book that contains all the marks that were granted to, and used by, the individual operative masons from around 1600. Another record of early Mark Masonry in late eighteenth-century Cornwall contains quite distinctive marks for each member. It was this practice which led to the degree of which we are now members becoming known by the name of Mark.

What is not so commonly known is that there were two other marks which were used amongst working stonemasons. The first of these was the 'mark of approval', signifying the accepted quality of execution, that was chiselled on the finished stone by the Overseer for that part of the building. This was a quite different mark from the personal one which such an officer chose when he too was admitted as a master craftsman or fellow. We still retain a trace of this usage when, after the Deacons have submitted their work for examination, each Overseer applies his tools to the cube and rectangle and symbolically makes a mark to the rhythm of the fellowcraft knocks. This is intended to convey, as the ritual states, 'Your work is approved and will be passed on to the builders'.

The second mark was one which we have totally discarded in Accepted Freemasonry. This was a mark that indicated where exactly any carved or approved stone was to be placed in the order of stones to be laid, particularly in the case of pillars, ribs or arches. The responsibility for such special marking lay with the master mason, or his deputy, because they alone were in possession of the scheme for the whole structure. The nearest we come to any such old custom is when the Worshipful Master says: 'I well remember issuing the design for such a (key)stone.' He reminds us that every stone was intended to be made for a particular purpose and so had to be marked accordingly. Mark Master Masons would be those who traditionally had this gift of further knowledge and the means to apply it for the benefit of subordinate craftsmen.

In considering this matter of multiple marks it may be puzzling as to why the latter two of these rarely seem to be visible. The answer, of course, is that whilst all the marks would be visible whilst the stone was waiting to be placed in position the one indicating its exact placement obviously disappeared as it was set in position on or amongst those stones already laid. The Overseer's mark could be on any side but was most likely not on the same side as that of the craftsman who made it if only to avoid any confusion. Since the marks of the craftsmen were usually displayed on the exposed face of the particular features so that it could be identified for repair, replacement or refinement if the mason or his son were still alive, it means that almost without fail the additional marks never receive the attention of those who, as many have done in the past, make a point of collecting masons' marks found in ancient buildings.

What has often been remarked on is the evident succession of family marks found on the walls of a cathedral or minster as it was slowly erected. The mark was the medieval equivalent of a present multistore logo. Whilst no longer a mark with peculiar mathematical or esoteric meaning it still has a very personal reference that reminds us of our masonic past and inheritance.

3. The Keystone (or Plug)

One would have thought that there could never be any question in the mind of a Mark Master Mason about the significance of the keystone or, as it is still sometimes referred to, the Capestone. Once it has been declared to be missing and there is a likelihood of the completion of King Solomon's temple being delayed as a result, the Worshipful Master says those unforgettable words: 'It is the most important stone in the building. Richly rewarded shall he be who succeeds in discovering it.'

The full importance of the keystone in the whole fabric of Freemasonry is, however, sadly diminished for most Mark brethren today because of the alterations that have taken place in our ceremonies.

In the earliest forms of the Mark rituals the candidate was either told how the keystone was placed in the final and principal arch of the temple of Solomon or he was actually directed to carry out such an act. There even grew up, in Irish and military lodges, a quite short but memorable ceremony regarding this, and in due course that became a degree in its own right. It is now known as the degree of Most Excellent Master which is regularly practised by Mark lodges in the United States of America and Canada. For anyone who takes part in it there, it certainly makes an indelible impression on one's memory and it also covers a gap that one can experience when pondering on the Mark ceremony in which we normally take part. I believe that we have lost a vital clue by omitting both the act and its explanation.

Earliest Mark Tracing Board of Albany Lodge, Newport, Isle of Wight.

In the 18th century the Mark Master degree was directly associated with the degree of the Holy Royal Arch, as is the case in Ireland and Scotland to this day, where it is both required by it and precedes it. As a result of separating these two connected stages of Masonry we have lost the awareness of how the keystone came to be in the Arch and why its use was so important. But there will yet be those who wonder what precisely the situation of this arch needing the keystone might be. The answer is that it was the arch that spanned the entrance to the Holy of Holies and over the curve of which was set 'the dormer that gave light to the same', that is, light for the door and its veil. It was thus in a most important and very sacred part of the building and when we know this it can perhaps be better understood why there was so much consternation when such an item was said to be missing.

The keystone is an architectural item that is produced by the use of the square and compasses in its design. Because we have removed any mention of the link that there once was between the Master Mason and Mark Master Mason degrees, save for the requirement that a Mark Master must have been through the 3rd degree, it is not surprising that we fail to see the connection with these working implements that are said, in the opening of a lodge in the 3rd degree, to be the proof of a true Master Mason and the work which he can then undertake. When we recall that the purpose of a Master Mason is to leave the East, where the porchway or entrance of the inner temple was, and to go to the West, where the Holy of Holies stood, we can even more appreciate why this crowning work of a Mark Master Mason was so essential.

What, of course, should never allow us to forget the keystone is the fact that as we greet each other we are to communicate first a grip which is meant to allude to 'the want of a keystone to complete the Arch' and then another to remind us of its normal position. The instruction in that act is so brief in the course of so much else that we are taught and shown in this ceremony that it is not surprising if, as Mark Master Masons, we easily overlook it.

It is worth mentioning here that whilst a keystone has a similar place in the working of our neighbouring Constitutions it becomes a different 'capestone' when it appears in their Royal Arch practice. There it becomes a plugstone that is the principal, holding-together piece of a dome. That dome was also associated with the Holy of Holies so its importance in the construction of the temple was just as great as for our own keystone. Why it is a 'capestone' for the dome and not the arch is not something we can explain here.

4. The Cornerstone

If there is one aspect of the Mark degrees which most often bemuses the thoughtful Mark Master Mason it is the confusion in this degree between a keystone and a cornerstone. I have tried to deal fully with the keystone in the previous talk in this book but it may help to resolve the puzzle about why we mention both types of stone if we realise that in the working trade of the stonemason there were two general divisions of work: those who dealt merely with what was called square or straight work whilst others were able to produce arch or round work. In the medieval trade the terms that were more commonly used were of quarriers and stone squarers in the first category, and carvers and moulders in the second. There were, of course, other masons who were known as layers and erectors but they need not concern us here.

Each of the workers in these two general grades were not only provided with their own special marks but also had to complete their own peculiar forms of 'masterpiece' – in the former group it was the perfect ashlar, a stone of true die or cornerstone. In the other group the masterpiece was a shaped pediment or keystone suitable for completing an arch or the crossed ribs in a roof. The perfect ashlar, by the way, did not just have to be square but could be rectangular, which helps us as Mark Masons to realise why three stones are usually submitted by the Deacons and the candidate to the Overseers. It may be worth pointing out here that in the preparation of the ashlar only a square, level and plumbrule are needed but to fashion the keystone a pair of compasses becomes essential. There is a tradition which states that an inn in which stonemasons of all skills would meet was given the name of 'The Square and Compasses' instead of the more common 'Masons Arms'.

In the earliest presentation of Mark degrees there are already the grades of Mark Man and Mark Master. It was then understood that in order to qualify as a Mark Man you had to have produced a satisfactory cornerstone whereas the shaping of a keystone was required for a potential Mark Master Mason.

It was because such a clear distinction was retained in the Mark ceremonies that the Mark degrees were, and by some still are, regarded as the most 'operative' of all the older degrees in Freemasonry.

The cornerstone is, of course, referred to in the Hebrew words that appear over the arched entrance that is shown on the Mark tracing board. They read as follows:

Eben	*mah-asu*	*hab-bonim*	*hay-thah*	*l'rosh*	*pinnah.*
A stone	*rejected*	*by the builders*	*became*	*as head*	*of the corner*

These words are first found in Psalm 118 verse 22 and have a quite legitimate Hebraic significance. They refer to what was believed to be an ancient story of how materials that were provided for use in constructing an edifice for God were at first wrongly rejected as unfitting but then later recognised as crucial for the work. This tradition was adopted by the Jews who were the first Christians, who applied it to their Lord and Messiah, Jesus, in the sense that he was also the one despised and rejected by men but in due time was recognised as the true source of life and light and the necessary cornerstone of a whole new temple. That is why there are so many similar references to this verse in the New Testament part of the Volume of the Sacred Law.

In a strange sense the rejection of the cornerstone is a metaphor for the underlying fact that a Mark Master Mason is being taught. He has to learn the lessons of patience and humility as he makes his way through the degree and in his progress through life. The fact that he may be misunderstood or even unjustly treated is one of life's hardest trials. The fact that this 'Mark theme' could be used to suggest a New Testament parallel may be helpful for some but is not to be thought essential. The Mark Master Mason learns that, like King David, he may for a time suffer judgement and rejection as a builder but God's ultimate plan was to vindicate this royal house and ensure that David's plan and offering would end up with the completion of the Jerusalem temple. A Mark Master Mason may be led to remark, 'Alas, Alas, my labour is lost' but he will happily discover that the stone which he presented has become a key- and corner-stone for the whole structure.

5. The Tracing Board

The origins of that piece of lodge furniture that we now call a tracing board lie in the practice of the master mason, who was also the architect of the edifice concerned, of drawing outline tracings of the whole work or its details, either on a wooden board or, as can still be seen in York and Wells cathedrals, on the floor of a special tracing room. Because this 'drawing' was the essential means by which the master mason could communicate the building plans and its details to the foremen or Overseers it is clear that such a board has an obvious relevance to the story that we still tell in the Mark Master degree. To have a tracing board in a Mark Masons lodge room is a highly appropriate arrangement.

Following the establishment of the first Mark Grand Lodge in England it was to take thirty-five years for that governing body to make up its mind as to whether it would authorise an official tracing board. When, however, you consider that the influential members of the new Mark body were themselves also prominent Craft Masons and no steps had been taken in their Grand Lodge to agree on the styles of board for the first three degrees it is hardly surprising that there should be a proper reluctance to commit this order to one design of Mark board. That is not to say that there were no boards before 1892 but not one of those earlier ones that were in use apparently so commended itself as to be acceptable to all the lodges that worked the Mark degrees. Even the board that was finally recommended, and which has now celebrated a centenary of use, is not the board that you will necessarily see in all Mark lodges.

The one, however, with which most Mark Masons are now familiar was designed by a Brother Arthur Carter and even its proposed acceptance by Grand Lodge was at first challenged just because there were those who claimed that it was being foisted on the Grand Lodge by the General Board without any opportunity being given for its consideration by the members of the Grand Lodge itself. It was eventually required that every Mark lodge should purchase such a board though, surprisingly, the lecture to be used in conjunction with this design was that which had been devised to accompany and explain a somewhat different and earlier board.

In the light of what seems to have been a somewhat confused solution it is significant that there are, as already stated, some lodges that simply retained the board that once went with the still authorised, if earlier, lecture. Such lodges never purchased the newer board. It is also a sad fact that there are lodges that have too few occasions on which an explanation of whichever board they may possess is given, as is the case with the board in the first of the Craft degrees. This means that the brethren are deprived of certain useful information about that Masonic step which they will have taken.

When the present board was at last introduced it was claimed that it was more colourful and attractive than its predecessors, that nothing had been omitted from such features as had appeared before and that all the essential items that related to the Mark were portrayed.

When you compare this new board, however, with, for example, the similar but older Rosenthal board, this is not strictly true. Where, for example, are the cramp, the twenty-four inch rule and the open Volume of the Sacred Law? The board shows border colours and design that suggest a link with the Holy Royal Arch with which, in England, the Mark degrees are not directly associated. Further reflection on the present board prompts other questions. What is the significance of the eight steps that lead from the mosaic flooring to the porchway or entrance and why are there only three rungs on the ladder? Are the two pillars meant to imply that the Mark is attached to the Fellowcraft degree and if they are the pillars of the inner sanctuary of King Solomon's temple then why are they inside an edifice which is then also shown as appearing in the distance? Why, moreover, is there no explanation of the old cipher alphabet that is at least represented amongst the symbols? It is when these questions are posed that you begin to realise how many parts of the tracing board are still left unexplained.

6. The Heave-over of the Keystone

In every degree of Freemasonry there are the critical moments which we are never likely to forget. They are moments when we are placed in a situation which may have made us wonder what it was that we had allowed ourselves to get into. One of those moments is when we at last stand in the North-East part of a lodge room and are invited to exhibit a benevolence that we cannot at that moment fulfil, much as we might wish to do so. A similar experience comes when we are standing in full view of all one's brethren and being asked to reply, unaided, to a set of questions that it is hoped you have learned correctly, though probably not understood. And the third degree has its own dramatic ceremony in which we might well wonder, as we lie entombed, wrapped or just exposed on the lodge floor, what is to happen next.

In the Mark degree there is a no less poignant moment. We are encouraged to submit an unusual piece of work which we have trustingly received in our hands but which is now being rejected with the somewhat unlikely words, '*Your* work is rejected' when in fact we had nothing to do with it. The surprise is certainly the greater because the first two people to inspect it, whom you hear called Overseers, were apparently willing to permit it. And then, to make the occasion even more painful you are asked to stand aside whilst the Overseers are questioned and then told to throw the stone that you brought amongst the rubbish. From first coming with the hope that your stone might, like the square and rectangular ones, be used to build the temple of Solomon, one's feelings are probably now confused and surprised. Confused because the reason for the stone's rejection is not really clear and surprised because it was presumably put in one's hands for good purpose in the first place.

What exactly is this act of 'heave over' that is still retained and partially re-enacted in the course of our Mark degree? Well, it is certainly something that formed a part of the earliest speculative rituals to which we have access and so it is by no means a late invention or bright idea. The only major difference from earlier practice is that in an original Hebrew tradition it was not the stone that was rejected and heaved over an edge but the workman who had produced such a faulty piece of work. I mention an 'edge' because it should be remembered that the Jerusalem temple was built on a mound above the city and so there were steep drops on all sides of the site, as indeed there still are.

At least we have to be grateful that by the Middle Ages it is the stone that was carried from the site on a bier, as if it were a dead and useless person, and then tipped over to be amongst the rubble.

In Jerusalem, as this rubble was in a valley beneath the walls, where the common refuse of the city was also deposited, it meant that when any workman was punished by being tossed over he was more than likely to be maimed, if not killed, by the fall into such a spot. We are also spared the medieval custom of a beating upon the head and back that any such inefficient workman received from his fellows for producing a bad example of the work by which they were all judged, and for wasting a good piece of stone for which they all shared the cost. Even that latter penalty we are now spared.

It is because of this that the earlier Mark rituals all mention a precipice over which the unspecified or spoiled keystone was to be discarded. Since such a stone was most unlikely to have survived damage after its 'heave over' it was assumed that another stone would now be required to be made in the quarries by a candidate so that he would have something new to present. That extra stage of work was no longer included in the revised ritual under the Mark Grand Lodge even though the 'heave over' practice was retained. What happened next is described in another of these talks. What we have lost in our present form of working is the sense of the severity of the punishment for work which, though not actually incorrect, is treated as such because of an apparent lack of communication among the Overseers.

Sitting disconsolately aside with, as I was first taught, my head laid on my right hand, is nothing like as severe an experience as it once was but it is still a moment to remember. As one senior Mark Mason once remarked, 'perhaps we are to learn that our work, however sincere, is not always appreciated as we might think it should be'.

7. The Search for the Stone

When we have reached the high point of our ceremony, where the consternation caused by the failure to produce the needed keystone has reached its peak, the Worshipful Master, as we know, addresses the members with these words: 'Let diligent search be made for it. It is the most important stone in the building'. Why it is so important has already been considered in one of the other talks in this series.

It has to be said that I can well recall the real search that I was encouraged to make fifty years ago before ever my attention was drawn to where the stone may have been finally lodged. If there is one portion of the Mark Master ceremony in which it has been possible to reveal real change in traditional practice within one Mark lifetime it is at this point. Previously it was often the case that the stone was moved discreetly from where it had apparently been left at the heave-over as if it had continued rolling into another location. It did therefore need looking for by the Senior Deacon and the candidate, peering here and there around the room and having to look carefully to find it. Today the rubric referring to the search assumes that as a candidate sees where the stone was previously left, such a pretence of looking for it is both foolish and time-wasting. Something that can be seen as more sensible and direct by way of recovering the discarded stone is recommended.

Yet if this is to be our present practice one is bound to wonder why the clear directive of the Worshipful Master is also retained. Why mention a search at all? The answer surely has to be because whatever the current straightforward logic of the present suggested practice, the real origin of this practice cannot be so easily dismissed. Let me explain to you what I mean.

In another talk on the 'heave-over' I attempted to explain that what was being symbolically represented – that originally a stone, instead of the workman whose work it was, was literally thrown over the deep sides of the temple mount at Jerusalem and fell onto the rubbish or rubble in the valley below. There are even old rituals that describe this drop as being of some 30 feet or more and there was an understanding that this was in a valley called Gehinnom or Gehenna beneath the eastern walls. This place was where the city piled its refuse, and because it was always burning the name Gehenna became an eventual name for hell, which was thought of as a place of perpetual burning.

It is at this point that a distinct difference is to be noted between the working stonemasons' practice of disposing of a stone that was badly made or damaged and the story that we tell, of how a stone that is recognised by the

Overseers as being well executed yet is not in accordance with the plans that they appear to have received. When the real explanation of what happened, as stated in our version, is revealed it shows that searchers were urged to make their way symbolically down the steep side of the mount by a circuitous path in order that a diligent search could be made for what it was hoped was still an undamaged and usable keystone. That kind of circuitous path around the lodge room in the search was what older Mark Masons were introduced to. It was certainly not meant as a foolish waste of time but the re-enactment of the real basis of the discovery of the most important stone for the building. What may be of interest to some Mark Masons who have made further progress in their Masonic journey is that in some West Lancashire Royal Arch Chapters the path that the candidate first takes around the chapter room is identical with the circuitous path to which I have alluded above. As that chapter path leads to the discovery of the restored keystone, and since the Mark degree anciently was required before the Royal Arch ceremony, as is still the case in Scotland and Ireland, the northern practice fits the old custom perfectly.

It is of course true that many traditions in our Masonic practices have been omitted and even lost, or have been taken up into other degrees of which Mark Masons may never have the opportunity or desire to be aware. What seems a pity is that if Mark Masons today are still being urged to make 'diligent search' for a discarded stone they ought at least to be given an informed explanation why such a search is necessary when none is in effect made and what it was that led to the idea and the instruction in the first place.

8. The Overseers

The term 'Overseer', and the work that such an official in the stonemason's trade was expected to do, is not something that the normal Freemason today would be at all familiar with. Any brother who has experienced the Craft third degree can perhaps recall that at a significant part of that ceremony there is a mention of 'the Menatschim, or more familiarly speaking, the Overseers' who play a quite decisive part in that degree's story. The fact is, therefore, that Overseers appear on the Masonic scene before any brother becomes a candidate for the Mark. If, however, any Mark Master Mason were to be asked today what he might regard as the distinguishing characteristic of this order it is more than likely that he would mention the presence and work of the three quite separate officers called Overseers. It may, therefore, come as something of a shock to discover that in the earliest days of English Mark Masonry, and until the second decade after the establishment of the Mark Grand Lodge, these officers were either just not present or were not considered as really required.

Why this was so is not difficult to explain because the earliest examples of anything that might be recognised as the Mark degrees are found in the practices of Irish, military and Antient lodges and in these bodies the ceremonies were conducted as part of the normal Craft lodge procedures and under the same Craft warrant. Since the three acknowledged principal officers there were the Worshipful Master and his Wardens so the office of those who checked the credentials of the craftsmen, and the acceptability of their workmanship, was naturally that of those who were responsible for the normal governing of the lodge and its members.

That this was the original arrangement and the pattern of traditional practice is reflected in the content of our present day ritual where it is stated that whilst 'the Overseers were selected by our Master to aid in the work confided to HIS care' it is still the Wardens who control the payment of due wages for all deserving work and it is they who exact the penalty from any workman who tries to claim false wages for a lower rank.

The ancient situation is even more strongly supported by the old working that we find in a Midlands Mark lodge that can trace its origins back to pre-Union times. In this lodge the apparent anomaly of two sets of rulers was overcome by relinquishing the offices of Worshipful Master and Wardens and replacing them for the purposes of the Mark ceremony with a Worshipful Master Overseer, a Senior and a Junior. They, at least, are trying to be logical if, as the ceremony seemed to require, they had to have Overseers.

If, therefore, we realise that Overseers were not at first needed as another distinctive set of officers, and in the practice of the Mark degree in Scottish Craft lodges that is still the case, we will not also be surprised to learn that not every Mark lodge has them seated together in the centre of the lodge room. When such officers were at last recommended as a normal part of Mark practice they sat, as the first lodge Deacons did, behind or beside their senior counterparts, or, in some instances, immediately in front of the Worshipful Master and Wardens. In the Minerva lodge of Mark Master Masons that met in Kingston-upon-Hull, this latter position is where the Overseers sit to this day. Interesting, isn't it?

There is another aspect of the work of the Overseers that can be so easily overlooked by Mark Masons. Their examination of the stones that are presented to them, and their need to consult the plans for such stones before they can be passed on to a superior, is not all that has to be done. Before the stones are fully accepted for the work of building the temple the stones have to receive a distinctive mark that shows that they have indeed been presented at the 'gates' of the Overseers. In another talk in this series it was pointed out that there was not just one mark but three on an approved stone. The second of those marks was the one we have just described. It was the mark of approval from the foreman, or Overseer, who had charge of a number of the craftsmen. It is in a very real sense the rightful claim of the Mark degree that it preserves in several ways the operative traditions of the ancient craft. The presence of the Overseers with their examinations, their plans and mark of approval, are all traces of that connection.

9. The Senior Warden's Wicket

The presence and significance of 'the Senior Warden's wicket in the West' as part of our ceremonies is meant to remind us of how closely related to the Craft our Mark tradition has always been. Yet because the second or Fellowcraft degree of our English Masonry is now generally described and thought of as simply 'passing', and accordingly as passing easily out of mind, we need to be reminded that in ancient Freemasonry it was the 'fellow, or master, of the craft degree' that claimed the place of pre-eminence and was the step by which the old traditions were specially obtained. This was the point when a mason ceased being an apprentice and at last became the maker of a masterpiece and hence a skilled workman in his craft who was now entitled to receive proper wages.

It was as a fellow that he showed his skill and was rewarded for his first practical application of some of the seven liberal arts and sciences. That is what the presence of the wicket is really trying to teach us.

It is not therefore surprising, and would be a fair deduction from what one has usually seen in most Mark lodges, that the brethren imagine that the wicket frame that sits on the Senior Warden's pedestal has always been such a permanent fixture of a Mark lodge. If that is what is still thought then it has to be said that we are sadly mistaken and misinformed. Both historically, and in terms of the ritual, the wicket is only meant to appear occasionally, to be used sparingly and for two parts of the Advancement ceremony only. It was for just this reason that Masonic furnishers devised the present item which can be so easily erected and dismantled. In the opening and closing ceremonies of the lodge, as well as during the conduct of the lodge's general business, the Senior Warden should not be hidden from the Master's gaze and certainly not with a shield that permits him to read, rather than recite, his parts of the ceremony. The wicket ought only to be put in place when it is required.

Earlier forms of the wicket.

As a number of photographs in this book make clear, the origin and development of the wicket support what has just been said. It began its life, as one current American ritual book makes plain, as the hole or aperture in the entrance door of the lodge, through which communication takes place with the tyler, and which happens also to be close to the chair of the Senior Warden. When its particular use in the Mark was needed the Senior Warden slipped out of the lodge room and stationed himself, as if in a paymaster's office, behind the door. In this position he was symbolically in that middle chamber of the temple about which we are informed in the explanation of the 2nd degree tracing board.

The distribution of wages then took place with the members lining up to approach the door, with the Junior Warden standing on the inner side of it. The tyler's flap, or if it was more convenient, another opening in the door was used for receiving the hands of the brethren. Before Deacons were introduced it was the Senior Warden who was expected to punish a fraudulent workman because the Junior Warden was the officer pleading the cause of the threatened candidate. That was, by the way, the usual role of the Junior Warden, as Conductor, even in Craft ceremonies.

In due course, and especially when lodges still met in taverns, it was preferred to have a separate 'door' with a lattice type surface and this was erected in the North-West part of the lodge room so that the Senior Warden could place himself behind it as the ceremony proceeded. Such doors still exist in some Scottish lodge rooms. Even when such a door was halved and lifted, as required, onto the Senior Warden's pedestal it resembled a door with a hole rather than the pointed wicket with which we are familiar today.

It was, as already stated, the advent of the regalia manufacturers that led to the production of the modern, handy gadget that could be so easily set on the Warden's pedestal. It is just because it can now be so easily handled that it need not be 'in situ' permanently. Its presence throughout the ceremony can suggest that its use is perhaps the focal point of the whole proceedings. That would be an assumption that is both unfortunate and misleading. In a quite literal sense the wicket needs to be kept very much in its place.

10. The Mark Master's Apron

If there is one item used in the Mark degree that might be thought to be of long established tradition it is surely the apron with which our members are invested. The truth, however, is that it is only in England and Wales, and those lodges that became their offspring overseas, that a separate Mark degree apron is both known and required. When you think about it you can soon see why this should be the case.

In Scotland the Mark degree may be conferred in a Craft lodge and in that case the officers and members are naturally dressed in their usual Craft clothing, as is the candidate. If, on the other hand, and as is also the case there, the degree is conferred in a Royal Arch Chapter then the companions wear the appropriate dress for that ceremony. The same is true for Ireland although there the degree is only conferred in connection with a Chapter. This reflects an 18th century practice of administering the Mark degree on the authority of a Craft warrant with the brethren all wearing the customary attire of Craft Masons.

It is true that as the 18th century progressed a custom developed of having aprons that exhibited symbols of all the degrees that the possessor of the apron had taken and in such cases that apron was worn in any degree in which the owner took part. It was this practice, that could so easily create an unhelpful spirit of distinction between brethren, that was strictly forbidden by the Duke

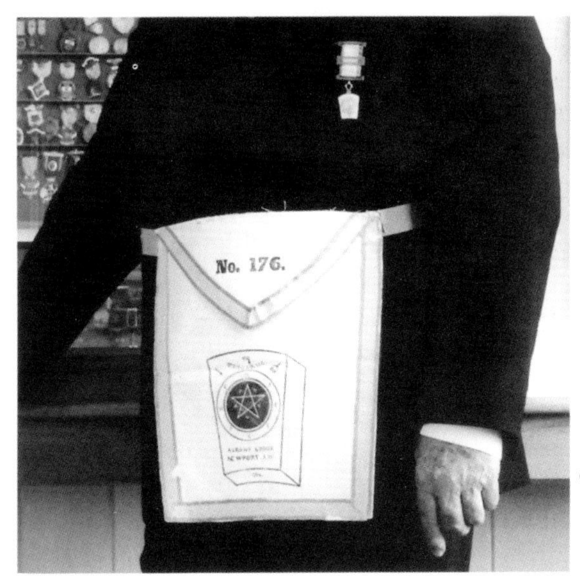

Close-up of earlier Mark 'keystone' apron.

of Sussex after the Union of the Grand Lodges in 1813. It was as a result of his initiative that the principle of wearing a separate type of apron for each degree was introduced, along with the requirement that no other degree symbols were to be shown than those of what was being worked. It was the unquestioned establishment of this principle in England by the mid-19th century that meant, with the introduction of a separate Mark degree, that consideration had to be given to the matter of what dress Mark Masons would adopt.

Where then did our distinctive and pleasing design of apron come from and why in such a style? The design was in fact created by a Scotsman, Brother Beattie, of the Aberdeen Royal Arch Chapter. The apron was first produced for the Bon Accord Lodge of Mark Masons which had been set up in London in 1851 by brethren affiliated to the Aberdeen Chapter, who were thus granted authority by that body to erect a Mark lodge. When, as has already been made clear, there was a close link between the Mark and Royal Arch in Scotland, granting such a step can be understood. That it was not understood, or appreciated, by many other English Freemasons is another story.

It was largely from the membership of the Bon Accord Mark lodge that the Mark Grand Lodge was formed and from 1856 they chose this combination of Craft blue and Royal Arch crimson that we find blending together so well.

It should be noted that this form of Mark apron was not the first style to have been adopted in previous Mark lodges in England. In the Isle of Wight, in Southwark and Nottingham there had been devised an apron with a 'keystone' shape and this was used in the first half of the nineteenth century. The need for this separate regalia arose because of the changes following the 1813 union and their firm implementation by the Provincial Grand Masters. They insisted that the previous custom of practising the Mark ceremonies in a Craft lodge must cease though they might continue at another time and place. As a result, the Mark bodies concerned had to start making some significant changes and additions to their former practice. Not only did they have to decide on what form of dress they should wear but they had also to devise a form of opening and closing what was now their quite separate stage of Masonic progress. When the Mark Grand Lodge had been established there would even be the need for their own form of installation for a Worshipful Master. The choice of a keystone style of apron was therefore ingenious as well as appropriate. That it was discontinued as an option following the formation of a Grand Lodge must have caused certain long-standing Mark Masons some heartache because such aprons had needed some skill and cost to produce. However, it has to be said that the shape, colours and symbolism of the present form do remind its wearers of the traditional links of the Mark with both the Craft and the Holy Royal Arch. That was no doubt much in the minds of those who authorised it.

The Importance of the Mark for Masonic Degrees

'Preaching to the converted' is a comment, and sometimes a criticism, that is quite often levelled at someone who shares my calling. It might indeed be a comment that is appropriate for such a gathering as this. For honoured as I am to address the members of the Mark Degree seated here I am quite sure that not a few of you could speak on the topic chosen. There are equally many more of you who would at least be very clear in your hearts as to why being a Mark Mason means that you are better instructed members, and perhaps better ritualists, in our English Freemasonry.

I am not therefore trying here to convince this audience of things that they do not already know or feel. Far be from me any such intention. What I am seeking to do is to put into some usable form what might be helpful ammunition for members to use when they may be challenged by those who are not yet of our number. For make no mistake, there are still many Freemasons around to whom anything beyond the three basic degrees, along with the installation of a Worshipful Master, is considered not merely unnecessary and intrusive but also quite irrelevant. They regard the Mark Degree, or even the Royal Arch, as an additional step which can be left, quite happily, aside. What then are we to offer if such opinions are expressed?

First and foremost we can properly claim that the Mark supplies answers to some of those parts of the Craft ritual that are either not fully explained or are just ignored. I will not, of course, be able to deal with all the items I could list under this heading because to do so would mean either a far too long lecture or that I cut out other headings that I do want to share with you. I shall therefore restrict myself in this section to just three examples.

In the present form of closing a Craft lodge there is one phrase that is too often repeated without giving it very much thought. It is the passage spoken by the Senior Warden, '...having seen that all the brethren have had their due'. What is that really all about?

Most Craft Masons today would, I suppose, say that it meant that we had got what we came for. If we came expecting an Initiation ceremony then that is what has been conducted and what was due to take place has happened. The correct explanation of this phrase, however, is much more interesting but needs a little unpacking in order to appreciate it.

The operative guild mason's ceremony of opening or closing a lodge was carried out in a lodge of Fellows, that is, those who were Freemen of the local borough, free, that is, of their indentures as apprentices *before* they could be admitted. It was within this lodge of Fellows, ruled later as a private lodge by a Right Worshipful Master and two Wardens, that the introduction of those who were not Freemen would have occurred. The proof of this is revealed by the fact that throughout most of the 18th century the Grand Lodge of All England at York admitted candidates in a lodge which was opened as a Fellows lodge and candidates were admitted as Apprentices *and* Fellows on the same occasion. Even after the York brethren stopped performing the two degrees on the same evening in 1780 they still only opened the lodge in one degree as Fellows.

The premier Grand Lodge of 1717 for London soon wanted to operate a separate Apprentice ceremony and so it adapted the opening of what they called a Fellowcrafts lodge and made it the basic opening practice of all lodges. It did the same with the closing. In doing this latter a problem was created since apprentices were never paid anything for they were provided with housing, clothing and food by the master mason to whom they were indentured. It was the fellows who were paid the wages that were their due.

At the close of the guild Fellows' lodges the Senior Warden, who was responsible for seeing that the Fellows were paid, was expected to report this fact to the ruling Master Mason but when this closing ceremony was transferred to what was a separate lodge of Apprentices the words were changed to 'the brethren have had their due'. Even to this day there are many English lodges, especially in the North of England, where the words used are, 'having seen the wages paid as they are due' and to confirm the fact the Worshipful Master further asks, 'And have all the wages been paid?' to which the Warden replies, 'They have, Worshipful Master, to the best of my knowledge and belief' even though no form of wages have in fact been paid. Thus do some of our Craft lodges retain a link with operative history without in the least understanding what it is that they are doing or why they do it. It is we in the Mark, with the Senior Warden's wicket, who ensure by our practice that the old tradition is retained and more properly understood.

What is more, you may recall in the Craft lecture on the 2nd degree tracing board (Emulation Ritual) a section which describes how the apprentices were provided with corn, wine and oil, that corresponds to their being fed and cared for by their masters. The craftsmen, however, were paid 'in specie' which meant metal coinage and that is why we still preserve the payment of a token or 'penny' at the wicket. Only we now know what is the proper 'due'.

We turn next to the so-called Traditional History of the 3rd degree where we meet these words: 'Fifteen Fellowcrafts of that superior class of workmen appointed to preside over the rest'. Just who were these brethren who suddenly appear from nowhere and yet become involved in one of Freemasonry's very significant events? I would not, I think, be wrong if I assume that very few indeed are those Craft Masons who would be able to give an answer. Of course there is an answer in the later part of that Traditional History but how many are those who connect the two sections? Even if the light dawns when we hear of the 'Menatschim or Prefects, or more familiarly speaking the Overseers, of which three of the same class could not be found' the query for any perceptive Craft Mason must be, 'Yes, but why these men and who exactly were they?'

Well, you do not need me to underline the fact that if such Masons had undergone the old operative custom of having their work scrutinised and checked by such officers, as is still our Mark practice, everything would be so much clearer. Here are the very Overseers who tested all work done by the craftsmen and who could thus assure the lodge members that a man knew how to make a smooth ashlar and was therefore eligible for those wages we have just mentioned. Moreover, some Mark Masons get excited about Masons' marks but I wonder how many of us realise that the medieval mason's stone had not just one mark but three: one by the man who prepared the work, one by the overseer who passed the work as satisfactory and one by the master mason or his deputy to indicate where and how the stone was to be placed so as to fit into the whole structure. And there is more on this point.

When you learn, as we Mark Masons do, that Grand Master Hiram had a master plan for the Temple to which only he and certain others were privy, and which had not been shared fully with the Overseers, hence their confusion after his death, the Traditional History begins to fall more into place. Seeing that it is three of these Overseers (and notice that it is three) who seek to obtain that secret 'by any means', it makes sense.

Thirdly, I turn to the 3rd degree tracing board. Many Craft Masons imagine that by the time the usual explanation of it has been given all that needs to be known about its contents has been imparted. Such is not the case. What must strike the attention of any intelligent observer is that on the majority of such boards there is a plaque either above the emblems of mortality, or as a panel

Another early Masonic apron with various symbols but revealing the Mark keystone.

below them, which bears an odd form of writing. No one, in my experience, normally explains in lodge either what those strange coded letters mean or why they are there in this unusual form on a Master Mason's board. It is true that the formula '3,000 years after the creation of the world' is spoken so that the figures on the board might make some sense but no reason is given why they are back to front.

The answer only becomes possible with our entry into the Mark, though it has to be said that few Mark Masons are given the introduction to this peculiar cipher alphabet that was much more common in my early Mark days, fifty years ago. Yet it is only in the Mark Degree that this very distinctive form of old Masonic writing has its proper place and it is here therefore that we hold the key to this Craft feature. As Canon Tydeman once wrote, 'The Mark Degree logically precedes the Master Mason's since it is necessary to study the key on the Tracing Board of the one (the Mark) in order to understand the writing on the other'.

You will now perhaps realise why I cannot prolong this section of my paper, much as I would wish to, but must pass on to some other points that need to be made. Most importantly our current Mark Degree contains in its ceremony two notable features that are essential to the best understanding of our English Freemasonry. If at this point I begin to hint at some things that are still beyond the reach of some brethren reading this I at least hope that such an intimation will serve as a spur to other necessary Masonic progress.

I refer first of all to the Keystone which is not only a revelation, though a puzzle, to the Overseers but is finally acknowledged as the chief stone of the building. In some older forms of the Mark degrees in England, and still in some forms of the degree practised in other lands, the final acceptance of the stone is accompanied by the words, 'and will be placed with proper ceremony in its rightful place in the Arch'. The mere absence of such words need not matter unduly, for anyone with any intelligence should be able to deduce that the only place for the chief stone to be set is as the cape- or head-stone of an arch. As we in fact say, 'without it the work is at a standstill'. We are thus the only brethren in the whole of English Freemasonry who have the essential link that leads from the 3rd degree to the Holy Royal Arch.

Whatever may have been the experience of others I can only say that whereas I had been bemused at suddenly seeing an arch with a keystone in that Order it was when I became a Mark Master Mason that the origin and significance of such a stone at last became clear. That is why, of course, it is still required in Ireland and Scotland that anyone wishing to become a Royal Arch Mason must first have taken the Mark Degree. It provides the natural and essential step in our system though I have to tell you that for me the North American 'Most Excellent Master' degree, originally called just 'The Arch Degree', is what perfectly completes our present Mark ceremony, and leads most naturally into the Holy Royal Arch. That we expect Craft Masons to jump at once into the Holy Royal Arch and make sense of it simply shows how much we have failed to realise how dismembered the original body of English Masonry has become. Being a Mark Mason repairs much, if not all, of that loss.

The other feature of the Mark that is essential, indeed I would say was invaluable, for all Freemasons is the theme that underlies our Mark Master ceremony. I can recall to this day how a grand old man of Surrey Mark Masonry, Very Worshipful Brother Bill Howes, drummed this great theme into my head at the meetings I attended as I rose through the various offices. Here in the Mark ceremony, he would repeat, we learn an important lesson for life in general. The lesson is that, however good our work may be, there is no guarantee that it will be appreciated for what it is or what it has cost us. In every Masonic ceremony there is a moment of crisis or shock when we, as candidates, are brought up short with some unexpected turn in the proceedings. Just remember standing in the North-East corner of the lodge room and being asked, in full view of strangers, for money you haven't got. That sort of experience is purposely reproduced in every degree and in the Mark, as we are all well aware, there is the moment when, to our surprise, our 'work is rejected and ordered to be heaved over'. We sit, or are meant to sit, disconsolate and learn the bitter lesson, 'My labour is lost'. That is an essential, if hard, lesson for us to accept in our progress throughout Freemasonry.

For just consider, I work and work and I cannot get to the Chair any quicker. I have laboured as a Worshipful Master and a Past Master and just look what Provincial rank I have been given. I have dedicated myself to Masonry for thirty years and more and still I just don't seem to be able to get Grand Rank. Haven't you heard such things said? Have you even thought such things in your own heart? Then, brothers, just sit and watch and learn from *Mark* Masonry. We don't all get the results we think we are due; yet if, as was the case in English Mark Masonry in earlier times, you were sent back to the quarries to prepare another work, your goal and service can still be recognised. But oh, what a service this degree does to Masonry in general by teaching some of its members this salutary lesson. I know quite a few brethren who would really benefit.

There remain three other points that I want to share with you before I end this presentation. First, there is the obvious one that becoming a Mark Mason not only enhances our understanding of the Craft but can make us better exponents of the Craft ceremonies by enabling us to practise some very similar ritual. Especially is this so if it is during the time that you may be climbing the Craft ladder or waiting for your turn to do so. Of course it helps if you treat Mark ceremonies with the same respect as that which is expected of those in the Craft lodge. Learning by heart is as essential here as it is in the Craft and it does nothing for any of us if we think that the Mark work is a soft option. Nor should there be any soft option behind the Senior Warden's wicket. If we really believe that the Mark is important for the rest of our Masonry we need to see that its ritual is performed with not less, but even more, attention. What it certainly does is give some brethren the chance to try out a Master's Chair before they undertake that important task in its Craft setting.

Speaking of Installation leads me on to my next point. It is in the Mark that we learn more of Adoniram who appears so briefly in the Craft Inner Working, and this is hardly surprising because the ceremony of being installed in the Mark Chair is based on some of what was once called the ceremony of 'Passing the Chair' in the Craft. This was a ceremony that was introduced from the 1770s to enable any Master Masons who were not yet, or ever likely to be, ruling Masters, to gain the signs, tokens and words that made them effectively Past Masters. It can thus be said with reason that what is learnt in a Mark Installation is both complementary to, and was long essential for many in Craft Masonry. Not surprisingly, therefore, I have known brethren who have asserted that it is only when they have been installed in a Mark Chair that they have felt that they have fully occupied that office. And that brings me to my last point today.

When I set out on this lecture I did not attempt to define what was meant or intended by 'Masonic degrees'. I would now have to say that for me that phrase includes everything that was first hinted at in the Masonic History given in the Anderson Constitutions of 1723 and 1738. I am well aware that there are clever critics around today who regard his Historic section as both legendary and even laughable. What we think of it, however, is not really relevant. What matters is how 18th century Accepted Freemasons regarded it and for them it was clearly a quarry from which the building bricks for many degrees were obtained. Accordingly we have there the materials for not only the Craft and Royal Arch, but the Royal Ark Mariner, the Knights Templar, the Royal and Select Masters, most of the Allied Degrees and even the Operatives. What is relevant to our subject is that in what we now call 'these appendant orders', save only the Knights Templar, it is still required that for entry you must be a Mark Master Mason. Even in the case of the Templars, the remarks I have already made about the Royal Arch, which is a requisite for those knights, suggest that being a Mark Mason makes that step invaluable. To be a Mark member is in a most practical sense essential for sharing in most of present Masonry.

First Worshipful Master in Newport, Isle of Wight, wearing Craft clothing with Royal Arch and Mark jewels.

I must not prolong this address. I hope that by what I have offered here we may all feel the more confident as we suggest membership of this Degree to those who are likely to prove good Mark Masons. What I also hope is that it may have reinforced our determination to understand and to practise our Mark Masonry because we have seen its relevance to the larger Masonic field. I can only close by saying: 'May Mark Masonry continue to flourish amongst us, making us better Masons overall'.

Interesting current variations in the Mark Degree

When the first Mark Grand Lodge was established more than a century and a half ago there was, no doubt, one proper wish of its experienced and very distinguished founders. This was that the type and practice of Mark Masonry, which they were now responsible for directing in England and Wales, might be uniform in all the lodges that would henceforth owe their allegiance to the Grand Lodge. Such had been the fervent hope of the Duke of Sussex forty years earlier when the United Grand Lodge of Free and Accepted Masons was formed. Yet the result in both cases has turned out to be somewhat different. In the case of the Craft there are now several well-recognised and accepted variations of working, if one mentions only those of Emulation, Taylor's and Universal. In the case of the Mark ceremonies the fact is that there had been, in the century prior to 1851, a number of lodges in England that practised their own forms of Mark Masonry and it would have been understandable if some of these older units wanted to hold on to their tried and treasured ways. In what follows it will be seen how far something of what they valued has been maintained even into the 21st century. For those who now have, or have had, the privilege of visiting around our land it must be said that such variations as remain make such an experience an added delight, as indeed is the case with visits in Craft Freemasonry.

The Newstead Mark Lodge in Nottingham once used an old form of working that they are still willing to demonstrate by arrangement. Though they have adjusted their own current working so as to conform largely with the more usual ritual they have retained some of their own practices that reveal their proud Time Immemorial status. I quote from the section prior to the obligation: 'The method of advancing to the East in this degree is by nine steps: the first THREE in the form of a triangle, stepping off with the right foot; the last SIX, bold or marching steps, stepping off with the left foot.' The partial similarity to the Ark Mariner and Master Mason degrees is striking.

When the members of this lodge conduct the presentation for inspection by the Overseers of certain finished work the Senior Deacon carries out his visit on his own, followed by the Junior Deacon on his own and it is only then that the candidate, carrying a keystone and accompanied by the Senior Deacon, is led to the gates of the Overseers for his separate presentation. That some such form of procedure was the usual older practice seems to be confirmed by the fact that certainly in my time as the Provincial Grand Master of Surrey there were some Mark lodges in which the Deacons made their visit to the Overseers separately, *before* the candidate made his own perambulation, guided by the Senior Deacon.

Returning to the Newstead Lodge, and the moment of the heave-over, the Deacons make four swings before the keystone is released, and the one who receives the stone 'secretes it and later hides it'. This means, of course, that there has to be a proper search for the hidden stone, which is then found, preferably, as the old ritual states, in the North-West, away from where it was apparently deposited. This is certainly the practice in the Royal Cumberland T.I. Mark lodge at Bath where the stone is taken to the furthest west of the temple and its eventual recovery is followed by the candidate being made to jog briskly to the Worshipful Master with his discovery. There are those of us who can recall when something like this usage was the normally accepted one.

Whilst we are with the Bath lodge it is worth noting that when the candidate is despatched to the quarries to prepare some work for examination he is instructed to roll up both legs of his trousers as the quarry area, he is told, is likely to be very muddy.

In the case of the Mark Lodge T.I. in York there is a feature that particularly merits our attention. This has to do with their use of music. We are all bound to be familiar with the opening and closing odes in some form or other and with the singing of a hymn during the members' symbolic progress to receive their wages. There are, of course, other rubrics in the ritual regarding possible chants in our ceremonies but we are not accustomed, as in this lodge, to there being a printed music book with words and notation for use by the brethren. This is surely a timely reminder to the brethren there, if not to other Mark Master Masons, that this aspect of our ceremonies is meant to be conducted with more than the usual attention. What is of special interest is the provision of musical accompaniment for other places in the ceremony than the ones with which we are usually acquainted. In all there are in York eight such chants and with the appropriate music for each. These are:

1) before the advancement prayer;
2) while the candidate is moving to the South-West;
3) during the sealing of the obligation;
4) after the heave-over;
5) during a search for the lost stone;
6) before the first sign is given;
7) before the second sign;
8) before the candidate is clothed with his apron.

Whilst the wording for some of these moments is clearly recorded in the authorised ritual, others, of course, are not. Such is the one that is sung as the obligation is being sealed:

> 'That which is gone out of thy lips thou shalt keep and perform. According as thou hast vowed unto the Lord Thy God'.

It is fitting to mention here that there are some Mark lodges in the Midlands that have other chants which vary from those just mentioned. This is the case in the Bath lodge to which reference has already been made. As in York, a Ceremonial Music book is available for those present and in their case the chants amount to twelve. In addition to the York ones there are chants for

(a) the approval of the mark chosen;
(b) before *and* after the obligation;
(c) when the candidate is moving to the Senior Warden for final presentation; and
(d) after the candidate has been invested with his apron.

What has also to be noted is that the opening and closing odes are completely different from those elsewhere.

To give a feeling of the variations used we might note that at the point when a candidate is being conducted to the Worshipful Master of approval of the mark chosen, the words in the York usage are: 'And he causeth all both small and great to receive a Mark in their right hand'. In the Midland working the wording is: 'It is your reward for your service in the tabernacle of the congregation.'

At the point of the heave-over the York Mark Masons sing: 'Hear me, O Lord, for Thy loving kindness is good. Reproach hath broken my heart and I

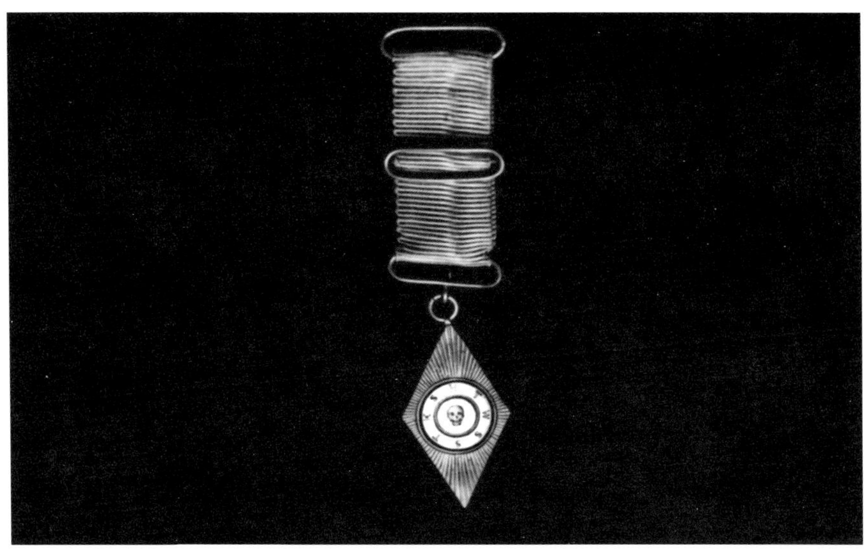

Early 19th century Mark breast jewel.

am full of heaviness. Hide not thy face from Thy servant for I am in trouble. Dishonour and shame have covered my face. Let Thy salvation, O God, set me up on high', whereas the words at Bath are simply: 'Have mercy upon me, O Lord, for I am in trouble'.

There are three other chants in the Midland version that are totally different from the York procedure. A new chant is used after the entrusting of the secrets and whilst the new Mark Master Mason is being conducted to the Senior Warden for investiture. Here we have: 'Except the Lord build the house they labour in vain that build it. Except the Lord keep the city the watchman waketh but in vain.' There is another new chant following the address after investiture: 'By this I know that Thou favourest me because mine enemy doth not triumph over me. And as for me Thou upholdest me in mine integrity and settest me before Thy face for ever. Blessed be the Lord God of Israel, from everlasting to everlasting. Amen.' The third extra chant comes at the close of the ceremony when the new Mark Mason is told that he may take his seat in the lodge. The brethren sing: 'Glory be to thee, O Lord most high.'

In the Old York Lodge, Time Immemorial that meets at Cleckheaton in west Yorkshire, an almost completely opposite practice to these is followed. There is no singing apart from the opening and closing odes, and the processional hymn whilst claiming wages. Elsewhere the rubric, and here it is in red because that is what the word 'rubric' means, says: 'The Chaplain delivers' and the words of Scripture are not sung but duly read by him.

When in this lodge the candidate is told to proceed to the quarries another rubric says that 'On the way the Junior Deacon collects ashlars from the Junior and Senior Wardens' pedestals.' Since the stones on those pedestals are usually the rough and smooth ashlars this hints at a real variation but that is not so. When the ashlars appear for inspection we see that they are the usual ones of square and oblong design so one presumes that these are the ones that were placed on the pedestals in this lodge.

The rubric regarding a candidate's choice of stone at this point does suggest something of a dilemma: 'The Deacons should *casually* allow the Candidate to choose which stone he will carry back into the Lodge, but *make sure* he takes the Key Stone. If this is done the following part of the ceremony has more impact on the Candidate' (emphasis added). Whilst this is a true conclusion, how to ensure that the right stone is the one selected may be more tricky.

In the following inspection the Overseers never apply their tools to the keystone because, says another rubric, 'it obviously is neither square nor oblong' and when, at last, the Master Overseer requires that the stone be heaved over among the rubbish he yet hands the stone back to the candidate who is led to the south of the lodge where the Deacons take the stone from him and 'heave it away'. As he sees this happen the candidate is told to repeat the words 'Alas, Alas, my l.i.i.v.' (labour is in vain) that I have never heard elsewhere. Reverting briefly to the same moment at Bath the candidate there at this point says *nothing*. He is left utterly bereft.

The candidate's subsequent request for wages having been incorrect, the Senior Warden cries, 'An impostor. Off! Off!'. And the rubric fascinatingly states: 'Senior Deacon blocks the Junior Warden positively. This is (however) a symbolic piece of ritual and not a trial of strength'.

In the conveying of the signs there is a clear use and explanation of the extended hand displaying the Sign Manual, as the first and not least important of the three; whilst at the closing there occurs a usual piece of West Yorkshire wording for after the phrase, 'it is closed accordingly', the Junior Warden continues: 'In the meantime, let us conduct ourselves in our several stations with credit to ourselves and honour to Mark Masonry'.

It is, however, when a Mark Mason visits the Minerva T.I. Lodge in Kingston-upon-Hull that some even more striking variations make their appearance. The visitor will notice at once, as he would if visiting in Ireland, that the Overseers are not found in their usual central positions but are seated in front of, and with their backs to, the principal officers. This surprise is at once followed by the words of the opening dialogue. The Worshipful Master addresses the Inner Guard as follows: 'Brother [A.B.], are all the Brethren assembled?' to which the Inner Guard replies: 'All the brethren are assembled, Brother [C.D].' The Worshipful Master then requests those present to assist him in opening a lodge of Mark Master Masons. What then occurs in no way complies with what we will usually expect. When the Junior Warden has reported the lodge being properly tyled the Worshipful Master asks: 'With what is it tyled?' to which the Junior Warden gives the answer: 'With secrecy and brotherly love; also by a brother of this degree without the door with a drawn sword in his hand.' The Worshipful Master: 'His duty there?' Junior Warden: 'To keep off all cowans and intruders and to see that none pass or repass except such as are duly qualified and have permission from the Chair.'

The wording is here consonant with Minerva Craft lodge ritual and serves to underline the fact that originally the Mark degree was part and parcel of their usual Craft working. Not surprisingly, therefore, as the Worshipful Master calls everyone to order as Mark Master Masons, he continues: 'Brother Senior Warden what is the situation of the Inner Guard?' and the Inner Guard responds for himself as do also the Deacons. Their responses are similarly of interest. When asked for their situations the Deacons each reply: 'Within hail of the Senior Warden (or Worshipful Master)' whilst in response to 'Your duty?' the Junior Deacon says: 'To carry messages from the Senior Warden in the West to the Junior Warden in the South and elsewhere about the lodge as he may direct' and the Senior Deacon, in addition to carrying messages, is 'to assist at the reception and advancement of candidates'. All this happens before we have mention of the only officers whom we normally mention.

In this lodge the Junior and Senior Overseers 'receive all materials brought up for the building . . .' whereas the Master Overseer 'presides at the inspection of all materials brought up' and 'if disapproved to call a council . . .'. If these are but modest alternatives the responses of the two Wardens are noticeably different:

> Junior Warden: 'As the sun is in the South at high noon, which is the glory and beauty of the day, so stands the Junior Warden in the South to call the Craft from labour to refreshment and from refreshment to labour as the Worshipful Master may direct.' The Senior Warden, when asked why he is 'so placed', answers: 'As the sun sets in the West to close the day so stands the Senior Warden in the West to assist in closing the lodge, to pay the Craftsmen their wages if any be due and to see that none depart dissatisfied,

harmony being the strength and support of all institutions, but more especially of ours'. The Worshipful Master's place is described thus: 'As the sun rises in the East to open and adorn the day so rises the Worshipful Master in the East to open the lodge and set the Craft to labour'.

The Worshipful Master then invokes the following blessing:

'O bountiful Creator, we acknowledge Thee to be our God. We bow before Thee, our King, we invoke and call upon Thee to be our helper in all our trials and difficulties. To Thee we owe whatsoever of good we possess; to Thee we look for every good to come. To Thee we direct our petitions, humbly beseeching Thee to protect our Queen, our country and our Craft, that so in conformity with the teachings of our Order we may continually by Thy faith be strengthened in hope and established in charity. So Mote It Be.'

The prayer having been rendered the Worshipful Master now, in the name of the Great Overseer of the Universe, declares this lodge 'open in due and ancient form for the despatch of business in the Mark Master Mason's degree'. To find such old practice still preserved is not just an interesting variation but sheds much light on our common heritage.

There are, of course, other features in the Advancement ceremony here. The Worshipful Master having ascertained the cause of a report gives permission for the Inner Guard to receive the candidate and the Junior Deacon says: 'Brother [candidate's name], having been regularly initiated into Freemasonry, passed to the second degree and raised to the sublime degree of a Master Mason now seeks for further light by being advanced to the honourable degree of a Mark Master Mason' and his help, besides those which we normally hear, is with 'the aid of the Mallet and chisel'. It is hardly surprising that in addition to the usual 'edge of the chisel' the candidate here is made to feel 'the pressure of the Mallet'. Facing the Inner Guard the candidate hears this: 'Brother, it is now my duty to place a mark upon you which you will probably carry to your grave'. He mentions the tools used on entry to the other degrees and then continues, 'The meaning of these symbolic actions were afterwards explained to you. In this degree you have a sharp chisel so applied to you that an indelible impression may be made. The mallet and chisel are instruments used in operative masonry to mark and indent the materials for the building, but in speculative Masonry we use them to mark and indent the mind'. He then applies the tools.

Proof of the candidate's being a Master Mason is given by the simple question, 'Have you attained that position?' and the reply, 'I have'. There follows a very short prayer humbly requesting that 'Brotherly Love, Relief and Truth may ever adorn our Craft' before the perambulation in which the signs of the three former degrees are exhibited.

The whole of the usual Mark Man ceremony is omitted and in its place the candidate at once takes an obligation. In this obligation he undertakes 'not to sell or exchange the mark, which shall be this night adopted by me, for any other, neither will I gage it a second time until redeemed from its former pledge ... should it not be prudent to (grant another's request) I will return him his mark with the price thereof or value to the amount of a least a quarter shekel of the Sanctuary... ' The vow is sealed on the V.O.T.S.L. four times, the book being open for two of the salutes and closed for the others. That done the candidate is told to go to the quarries to prepare a specimen of his work.

When the candidate re-enters it is with the Senior Deacon alone, the latter carrying a square ashlar and the candidate a keystone. They are announced as 'craftsmen from the quarries *of Tyre*'. On presenting the keystone at the South gate the Junior Overseer remarks: 'Place it in whatsoever position I may I find it impossible to adjust the angles ... Neither has it the mark of any of our Craft upon it. Is that your mark?' to which the reply is: 'It is not'. The procedure at the West gate is almost identical save that the Senior Overseer retains the square ashlar with the words: 'I congratulate you upon being justly entitled to your wages'.

At the East gate, therefore, *only* the keystone is presented for inspection and, after the usual rebuke, the candidate is asked to *stand aside* and the Senior Deacon is told to 'convey the stone to the *centre* of the building'. The command to have the keystone heaved over among the rubbish is carried out and the subsequent parade for wages ends with the usual consequence for the candidate.

The Worshipful Master is now informed of 'the want of a certain Keystone to the principal arch which no one has received instructions to make'. The search is made and after the stone is discovered the signs are given, but without any recitation of scripture passages. This instruction is very like the usual form save that the Hebrew words for 'Mark Well' are *Saroth* or *Kilroth* and the signs are in a different order. It is only now that the newly instructed Mark Master Mason is informed that *after* the ceremony he should approach the Registrar in order that he can choose an appropriate mark for himself.

There is no examination of the new Mark Master Mason before he is invested with his apron, after which the historical lecture is given. This contains the four sections below which are quite different to anything in the usually appointed lecture.

'In the previous stages of your masonic progress you have been placed respectively at the North-East and South-East corners of the lodge but you are now placed in the centre to represent the situation of our chief emblem, the Keystone.' The new Mark Master Mason learns that he formerly personified a craftsman who, according 'to ancient custom, on the evening of the sixth day of the week carried up his work for inspection'. This craftsman had 'discovered, in the quarries of Tyre, the Keystone to the principal arch of the Temple (although he was unacquainted with its use and value), deliberately laid aside his own work and took the keystone in its stead . . .'. The usual rejection and rebuke for seeking wages are described and the lecture ends with the words: 'The Keystone was then fixed in its proper position, the royal arch completed, and the Temple solemnly dedicated as a dwelling place for the King of Kings and Lord of Lords.' You might almost wonder which next Order your are in.

The next remaining variation is in the wording of the presentation of the working tools. 'The mallet teaches us to level every irregularity of conduct or temper that we may be the better enabled to exercise that pleasing acquirement – courtesy. Thus, what the mallet is to a craftsman so enlightened reason is to the passions of the human race. It curbs ambition, represses envy, moderates anger and encourages the noble soul'.

The Chisel, 'as the result of labour in removing (the diamond's) external coating, is able to present its latent beauties to our sight . . . [and like] discipline and education, develop hidden virtues of the heart and mind, which we as Masons are bound to exercise for ourselves, our Brethren and our God'.

In the closing the Senior Warden is simply asked the hour of the day, which is 'Past the sixth hour' and whether the craftsmen have been paid their wages. There is no mention of plans. The prayer is very brief and different and then comes this: 'Brother Senior Warden you have my command to close this lodge of Mark Master Masons and to dismiss the brethren from labour to rest until our worthy Brother of Tyre sends us a fresh supply of workmen and materials for the holy temple when I shall again claim your assistance and cooperation in the discharge of your respective duties'. It can, I think, be acknowledged that this, as the last variation, is a very distinctive one indeed.

Although there may be some other Mark variations that are not mentioned here it has, I believe, to be admitted that, apart from this notable example in East Yorkshire, in large measure the desire of the 19th century Grand Lodge founders for a uniformity in the conduct of the Mark ceremonies has been largely achieved. I was reminded, when talking with a member of the Albany Mark T.I. lodge on the Isle of Wight, of an early 20th century Provincial Grand Master there who made it his particular objective to remove every vestige of any older practice from the units under his control. What happened there has clearly been copied in Nottinghamshire and the far South-West where equally old lodges that had a distinctive Mark ceremony have them no longer. Whether that is altogether a blessing is for each Freemason to decide for himself. What I have tried to do here is to show some of the variations in England that still remain. If any brother wants to see further distinctive variations he needs to travel to Scotland and to Ireland. Describing the variations there is, however, another story.

A remarkable Peer and Masonic Leader

(Delivered in Leigh Lodge, No. 887 in 2006)

Lord William Henry Leigh, part of whose story I now have the privilege of presenting in this lodge that bears his family name, was a truly remarkable man. Not only was he the successor of a noble line that was already 350 years old, married to a wife from one of England's greatest families, a relative, if distant, of the celebrated novelist, Jane Austen, and one who left his indelible mark on English Freemasonry (forgive the pun) but he was also active in many fields of public activity. Of these latter it will be my pleasure to remind us in the time I am allotted. Our history as a nation, of course, is full of examples of men who employed their time and their gifts in a continuous round of public service and achievement. This Lord Leigh was indeed a member of that band.

His background was impeccable. The family rose to prominence during the Tudor age when Thomas, the son of Roger Leigh, a landed Shropshire gentleman, eventually became the Lord Mayor of London. He was apprenticed to Thomas Seymer, who was a member of the Mercers Company, and made free of his indentures in 1526, (the real origin, by the way, of why Masons still have to be 'free men'), was a merchant in fabrics at Antwerp in 1528 and soon after was wealthy enough to be able to lend a very substantial sum to the representative of Henry VIII in that city. Thomas returned to London, became himself a member of the Mercers Company, married the niece and heiress of the then Lord Mayor and lived in what was called a 'great mansion in Old Jewry'. In the years that followed he bought several properties in Gloucestershire in and around a place called Adlestrop and, being one of the king's commissioners for the closing of the monasteries in the Midlands, bought the buildings and land of Stoneleigh Abbey in Warwickshire.

After having been twice Master of the Mercers Company, and then an Alderman of the City, it was in the same year that Queen Elizabeth I came to the throne that Thomas became Lord Mayor and was made Sir Thomas Leigh the year following. It was as a result of these achievements that his son,

A silk picture showing Lord Leigh and Stoneleigh Abbey.

Rowland, was raised to the peerage as the first of the Lords Leigh, and from other members of this family subsequently no less than two famous Prime Ministers were produced, William Pitt and Lord Melbourne. The family was well and truly established.

The nearer predecessors of the Lord Leigh we are dealing with here created just the right setting for what was to be the exercise of his evident talents. His grandfather, James Henry Leigh, was the heir of a Reverend Thomas Leigh, rector of Adlestrop, who had no children. This man of the cloth had particularly cared for the estates that were attached to Stoneleigh with the result that the annual income from them circa 1800 had risen from £19,000 pa. to over £25,000. James's inheritance was thus substantial and the properties were also in good repair. It is true that the title had lapsed temporarily but James's mother was no less a person than Lady Caroline Brydges, daughter of the Duke of Chandos, and when James was 21 he took as wife Julia Judith Twistleton, the daughter of the 13th Lord Saye and Sele. It was this redoubtable lady who managed to gain a return to the peerage for their son, Chandos Leigh, so that our William Henry became the 2nd Lord Leigh of the new line. He was, in plain terms, born a nobleman with very promising prospects.

He was, from his birth in 1824, brought up with a clear understanding that he was to be the trusted owner of several Gloucestershire estates as well as being Lord of Stoneleigh. More of what that meant in practice we shall come to soon. After being schooled at home by a tutor he was entered as a pupil at Harrow and then went to Trinity College, Cambridge, where he gained a degree in law. At the age of 23 he stood as a local Liberal Parliamentary candidate, and though not then successful, he was soon able to make his political opinions felt because three years later his father died and the new Lord Leigh took his place in the House of Lords. He attended there regularly and his Liberal views were clearly known.

He also married. His choice fell on Caroline Amelia Grosvenor, a daughter of the Marquess of Westminster. Despite what we might regard as his eminent suitability as a suitor his future in-laws were somewhat doubtful of his credentials because of some publicity given to his father and grandmother regarding an earlier incident at Stoneleigh but so determined were the pair in seeking marriage that eventually permission was granted and a truly blessed union took place. They were to have 57 years together and produced ten children. Stoneleigh Abbey became a family home in a way that had never been the case before because William and Catherine were a true 'pater et mater familias'. That they were not only loving but loved is revealed by the enormous correspondence between parents and children which is safely preserved at Stratford on Avon.

This aspect of Lord Leigh's life is important because it underlines one of the elements of our Masonry that can be overlooked the more we become involved in our movement. Between 1681 and 1806 the Leighs of Stoneleigh had nineteen children of whom only eight survived. Thereafter, up to 1866, there were twenty-four children all of whom survived and for whom provision thus had to be made. If ever anyone took seriously the phase, 'without detriment to one's family or connections' that person was the 2nd Lord Leigh. His children were cared for and it is therefore hardly surprising that they both loved and respected their father.

As has already been hinted at by his involvement in the political scene after 1860 his Lordship adopted a practical interest in local as well as national affairs. I mentioned a little earlier that he regarded the ownership of his landed estates as an especial trust and this applied not least to the tenants who lived and worked on them. A survey carried out in 1883 showed that with 14,891 acres Lord Leigh was by far the largest landholder amongst the Warwickshire nobility. He was, as a result, the biggest employer of land workers and in the vicinity of Stoneleigh the only such employer. For him the protection and welfare of his workers was a constant care and from the start he took steps to acquaint himself with the details of each part of his possessions. 'He examined every account book personally, noting any discrepancy in the margin, prior to initialling each page' and adding his name to the half-yearly statements.

He made a point of visiting his tenants each year since he believed that it was 'not only desirable to see what they require but . . . to see that the cottages are not overcrowded with grown-up children, and kept clean'. He even inspected the kind of wallpapers that were used on their walls in case they too might be injurious to their health. In a collection of note books that he himself kept up to date for 43 years he recorded what repairs were required for each farm or cottage, plus the number and genders in each family. While showing care there was also an element of direction. All the dwellings had to be whitewashed every spring. Workmen were available to provide this for the old and infirm but any able-bodied tenants were expected to do it themselves with the materials being made available. The drains too were carefully inspected and had to be able to function effectively.

There were, as hinted above, rules about overcrowding. Any boy or girl over 16 was considered a lodger and lodgers were not allowed on the estates. Girls

The young Lord Leigh with his brother and sister.

were expected to go into service and the boys had to find work where separate accommodation was available. As both Lord and Lady Leigh once made clear: 'How horrified people would be if they happened to read in a newspaper that Lord Leigh . . . has a cottage in which he allows a father of three grown sons and two girls of . . . 14 and 10, together with a mother and several young children, together in a three room cottage. How can the commonest proprieties of life be observed in that house.' There are those who are involved with council estates today who might benefit by such wisdom.

Lord Leigh was no less interested in the state of the village school at Stoneleigh. It was not just a care for any repairs that might be needed but the competence of the staff and the standard of what they taught. Following the Education Act of 1872 some of his Lordship's previous concerns were met by law but he still donated an annual sum and supplied the classrooms with coal because he thought the local authority provision inadequate. His interest in education extended to the Craft. He was the Chairman of the Masonic Boys School and set up the Leigh Perpetuity Fund which enabled one Warwickshire boy each year to become a pupil. He was also a Governor and Trustee of Rugby School and acting as a local Justice of the Peace he was concerned about the education and welfare of many of those whose parents appeared before him. For boys who were themselves offenders he provided land at Weston-under-Wetherley for a Boys Reformatory with an annual nominal rent for 99 years. It catered for 90 boys who were taught various trades or were employed in cultivating the adjacent land. In 1884 three boys who had thus acquired agricultural skills were the first of many to be given jobs in Canada.

It seems that overcrowding in gaols, and the need for rehabilitation amongst prisoners, is again a problem for us. It was a concern for Lord William Henry. He regarded the gaols in Warwick and Coventry as 'schools of vice and depravity'. He was the one who introduced a motion for a single county gaol and in 1853 this was accepted. He was a member of the Visiting Committee for Prisons, and following his, as usual, carefully recorded experiences of prison environment, regime and treatment, he was the one who first brought about a change in the type of diet provided for inmates. Nor was that all. He was active in his concern for what happened to prisoners on their release. When he was told of such releases in advance he was often able to offer work on his estates or that of another landed gentleman who would accept his recommendation. We even hear of his securing an early release for one man so that he too could take up a job in Canada.

I made mention of the help the Leighs gave with the maintenance of their cottages when the occupants were old and infirm. It is noteworthy that Charles Booth, in his 1895 report on the national condition of the aged poor, specifically noted that Stoneleigh, Ashow and Westwood were exemplary parishes where the old were either provided with light work or were even pensioned by the landowner. Only one family, it was noted, had been removed to the workhouse and that was due to its own fault. A Friendly Society was set up in Stoneleigh in 1845 as William Henry came of age and it was by this means that local if modest pensions could be found.

It is further astonishingly recorded that even when his Lordship was abroad on holiday he would, on being told of an estate family's sickness, send orders for the housekeeper to provide the necessary food, or in one case a bottle of port wine. He is known to have given a regular payment to a man who had a mentally retarded daughter, and a recently widowed woman with four children was given a weekly sum, but, said his Lordship to his agent, that is not to be disclosed to the Parish poor relief committee because they help the children and this is just for her.

It may especially touch our feelings as Freemasons to learn that this care for others extended beyond his own properties and a ready supply of 5/- postal orders came by return to many who wrote to him asking for assistance when in deep distress. Like a true Samaritan he even instructed his land agent that if he would succour a needy tenant by paying a £1 coin out of his pocket his Lordship would repay him when they next met. Nor was this just another example of his care for local residents. In 1860 a treaty with France led to the lowering or, in some cases, the removal of the charges on certain imports of manufactured materials, so that, together with very severe winter weather, the ribbon weavers of Coventry were suddenly reduced to abject poverty levels. Lord Leigh, motivated no doubt by the genes of his merchant ancestors, headed a public appeal on their behalf that raised over £40,000. He also set up the Leigh Mills in Coventry to give alternative employment during such times of distress, and in his capacity as chairman of what was now the Coventry Emigration committee he helped many of the unemployed to find passages to Canada. A letter was sent from Liverpool in 1862 by a William Court. He stated that having been helped by his Lordship to get as far as that quayside he would lose his deposit if he did not sail next day but he was only to be allowed to take two of his five children with him. His Lordship immediately sent a cheque for £5 and the assurance of further help for the wife and other children after the husband's departure.

'Charity begins at home', however, was a common saying in Victorian England and it should not therefore surprise us to learn that it was not least to his household staff that Lord Leigh displayed the kind of care that we have already noted elsewhere. Their employer's care and goodwill was shown from House steward to the lowliest scullery maid and the esteem of the staff was expressed in return. His Lordship's birthday was celebrated by always including a servants' ball in which the first dance was led off by Lord Leigh accompanying the house-keeper and Lady Leigh partnering the butler.

Their wedding anniversary was also marked each year by a modest gift from the staff but on the occasion of their employers' Golden wedding the servants presented them with a silver reading candlestick and salad bowl. The staff appear to have been well aware that the daily family prayers were not merely formal but an occasion when the whole 'family' at Stoneleigh might recall in whom they should daily put their trust and learn right ways of living.

I like the picture drawn by the Lord's niece, Violet, in her autobiography: 'We sat up in the gallery [and] the small army of domestics below was divided into males on one side [and] females on the other... Uncle Leigh would appear and proceed to read prayers in a loud impressive voice and a dramatic manner'. The whole household was fully aware that the Leigh family motto, *Tout vient de Dieu* or 'Everything comes from God', was highly appropriate for a man who 'never doubted that God had created a hierarchical society and that such a society was necessary and beneficial'. Those, he believed, who were born with privilege were expected to serve and provide for those who were dependent on, if also below, them. William Henry fulfilled that calling.

There is the well-known story of how, when the house-keeper was showing visitors round the Abbey, which was opened occasionally without charge, she would, after pointing out several other portraits tell her audience, 'Now I'll show you the best man in England' and, sweeping aside a cover, would reveal a picture of the 2nd Lord. When this portrait was first presented to Lord Leigh by the County Council chairman he remarked that he was unaware of any man serving on so many charity boards who gave so few excuses for absence.

It would be remiss of me if I did not mention at this point one interest of his Lordship that was extremely common amongst his peers in the last 200 years. I refer to cricket. One of the most charming pictures of William Henry is when he was 18, showing him with a cricket bat over his shoulder and the stumps, two of them, held by his younger brother, the Honourable Edward Chandos Leigh. Stoneleigh Cricket Club was started by their father when William Henry was 15 and one of the oldest and most famous clubs in the county. William Henry persuaded his father to have a cricket ground laid out in front of the West Wing of the Abbey so that he could continue to play when he was not at Harrow. As the 1st Lord had played cricket with Lord Byron at that same school he was most agreeable to the suggestion. It was the younger boy in the picture who was to become the club's most famous player for not only did Edward gain his Cricket Blue at Oxford but he was to become a Gentleman, and later President, of the M.C.C. as well as Secretary of the exclusive club, I Zingari. The 2nd Lord not only rejoiced at his younger brother's achievements but also encouraged his own sons to play for the Club. On the occasion of the Lord's eldest son's 21st birthday the Gentlemen of Warwickshire celebrated it by playing an I Zingari eleven. Lord Leigh, I am sure, would have been very proud to discover that in 2004 Wisden's Annual was to describe the ground he had asked for as a boy, 'the loveliest ground in Britain'.

It was his combined sense of order and service that drew him enthusiastically to his royal and military commitments. He was High Steward of Sutton Coldfield for 23 years and Lord Lieutenant of the County from the age of 32 for the rest of his life. In the latter capacity he was host to Queen Victoria when she came to open the 'People's Park' at Aston in 1858. The cost of fitting and furnishing a suite of rooms for her personal use cost him some £6000, not to mention the sumptuous banquets which were prepared for her and the many guests on the two nights that she stayed at Stoneleigh Abbey. The facades of the Abbey and the gatehouse were illuminated by 20,000 lamps of varied colours and as this was at a date 50 years before electricity was installed at Stoneleigh the task of lighting the lamps was carried out by some estate workers during the time that the guests were at dinner. The Queen was duly impressed.

Of the military interests of Lord Leigh I have no need to speak at length because you have on another occasion heard separately the whole story of the Warwickshire Rifle Volunteers. It is here worth noting that the first steps towards forming a Rifle Corps were taken after a cricket match at the Stourbridge ground. Further progress was at first sluggish but when, Rugby and Coventry having formed units, Lord Leigh made it clear that when there were four companies he, as the Lord Lieutenant of the County, would appoint a Colonel, the Warwickshire Rifle Corps soon appeared complete. Having already been a Captain in the Warwickshire Yeomanry in the 1850s he became Colonel of the 3rd Battalion of the Warwickshire Regiment.

It was such a man as this, with all his many and demanding commitments, that we also know as a prominent figure in Freemasonry. To our order he clearly brought immense qualities as well as public esteem. That such a wealthy, principled and, not least, organised person should accept the positions he did both in his own county and the nation could only mean that Masonry in his care would benefit and flourish. In the book, *Marking Well*, that was produced for the 150th celebrations of our Grand Lodge I tried to point out especially Lord Leigh's larger contribution to the Freemasonry that we share. Here, in conclusion, we might perhaps centre on four brief snapshots of his involvement in the province of Warwickshire.

His remarkable rise from initiate to Provincial Grand Master in ten months was no mere flash in the pan. He was an active ruler for over 50 years and some 33 new lodges were consecrated in that time, most of them by himself. The story of Stoneleigh Lodge is one of those I like best. Lord Leigh, having received Queen Victoria's command to attend the ball held prior to the Princess Royal's marriage, the date of this lodge's consecration had to be postponed by three weeks. The ceremony was to be held in the King's Arms, Kenilworth, at 11 a.m., a church service at 2 p.m. and a banquet at Stoneleigh Abbey at 4 p.m. More than two hundred guests were in attendance, all in frock coats and top hats, and the brethren processed from the church to the Abbey. Dining was arranged for two hundred and fifteen, the Abbey chef had five more chefs from London to assist him, and the wine came from the Freemasons' Tavern in that city.

In 1876 the Provincial Grand Lodge met at the Town Hall, Nuneaton, with Lord Leigh presiding. A collection was made on behalf of the building fund of the new Abbey church there and £50 was provided. The Provincial Grand Lodge was adjourned as they proceeded to the site of the old Abbey church 'upon the foundation of which the Provincial Grand Master then laid the foundation stone of the new church'. When addressing those assembled there he said, 'I will again record the great gratification that it has afforded me and my brethren to take part in [this] ceremony. May I express an earnest wish that God may speed your work and that ere long we may have a church here which will be filled with worshippers of the Great Architect of the Universe'. How sad he would have been to note the antipathy to Freemasonry of many churchfolk today.

Attention was drawn last year to the interest which Lord Leigh took in the formation of the lodge that now bears his name whilst having some reservations about it being a lodge just for Warwickshire riflemen. Indeed he seems to have taken the opportunity of changing its name before he died. The same care seems to have guided him regarding the Mark lodges in this province for contrary to what one might have expected his Lordship, though being the first Grand Master of the new Mark Grand Lodge after 1851, was never a member of any local Mark lodge. This must have been determinate policy, reflecting the loyalty he owned to United Grand Lodge by not confusing a membership of a separate Order elsewhere with his duties to the Craft in Warwickshire. It simply underlines the principled nature of his behaviour and the thought he gave to the example he set as a ruler.

In 1870 the Provincial Grand Lodge was held at the new Masonic Hall, New Street, Birmingham. This was far from being the only new hall that Lord Leigh was to declare open for Masonic business. It was on this occasion that he described how he had received an anonymous letter casting certain aspersions on the conduct of a Worshipful Master in the province. He expressed his surprise and disappointment that any Mason should have written an anonymous communication and denounced the letter very strongly.

Such are just a few of the many varied situations in which this respected and remarkable man and a Mason found himself during this life of private and public service. The real contribution that he made in so many spheres is underlined by the unusual fact that when the day came for his body to be laid to rest in the Stoneleigh church mausoleum so many deputations from the bodies which he had supported wanted to be present that only twelve Masonic brethren, in full regalia, were able to be accommodated. At the same hour, however, two Masonic memorial services were held, one in the Cathedral at Birmingham and another in Holy Trinity church, Coventry, with present and past Provincial Grand Chaplains officiating at each. Lodges in the province were asked to forego banquets for one month and to wear black rosettes on their regalia collars for six. Countless boards and meetings must have stood in the customary period of silent remembrance of a most distinctive character. His contribution and example need long to be remembered, not only in Warwickshire but in Masonry as a whole.

Reconstruction of the Old Mark Degree workings

Part 1: Mark Man

Revised April 1986

Introduction

It having long been the wish of the then Provincial Grand Master of Surrey that there should be some means of enabling the Mark Master Masons to know the origins of their present ritual forms, and especially the distinction between the Mark Mason (or Mark Man) and the Mark Master ceremonies, the author requested permission to search afresh among the extensive archives at Mark Masons Hall and came across the documents which have enabled this presentation to emerge.

Broadly speaking the ceremonies now to be witnessed were first drawn together from old rituals in Mark Masons Hall archives and demonstrated as follows:

- The Mark Mason and shortened Mark Master at Sheffield in 1968.
- The Mark Master Degree in full at London in 1971.

The main differences between these two presentations were in the Opening and Closing of the Degrees and in the Charges that were appended to them. The variations have now been reduced to what may seem a more uniform style, though it should be emphasised that all the wording is from existing and early 19th century ritual sources and was therefore used at some stage in our Mark Degree development.

When the forms of ritual had been chosen in a way that would permit the separate parts to be performed as a connected whole, the other, and more important aspects of the enterprise became possible. These were to demonstrate how the present-day ritual draws upon its predecessors, how the Craft, Mark, and Royal Arch ceremonies were previously connected, and how certain symbols and ceremonies today have an explanation which has tended to be obscured in more recent times.

It will be noticed that there is a curious anomaly in the rituals which are here followed. The early part relates to the re-building of the Temple whilst

The obverse and reverse of the Mark keystone used by the Freemasons in the Minden XX Regiment.

the end of the Mark Mason and the whole of the Mark Master seem to relate to the construction of the First Temple. It seems reasonable to assume that this variation is due to early influence of the Scottish Royal Arch and the subsequent setting-up of the Mark Degree as a separate Order. It would be interesting to know when the 'Keystone of an arch' was substituted for what ought to be the 'Keystone of a Dome' since there is (at Great Queen Street library) evidence of the fact that this was at one time used as a 'Breast Jewel'.

It is also interesting to note that what is a categorical statement in the charge at the end of the present ritual is qualified in the older charge by the phrase 'While such is your conduct'. It cannot be denied that present ritual would possibly be enhanced by the inclusion of this older form.

The present reconstruction and its preparation in a form that could be presented at a special Mark meeting assembled for that purpose has proved to be both fascinating and rewarding. The brethren who have volunteered to take part will enable their fellows to further their interest and knowledge in the Mark Degree.

The ceremony that is to follow is not short and therefore some curtailment of its Craft setting has had to take place and the narration will describe certain ceremonies that cannot be shown in full.

The Order of proceedings is as follows:

A Craft Lodge will be declared open in the 1st degree.
A Craft Lodge will be declared open in the 2nd degree.
A Mark Masons (Mark Man) Lodge will be opened.
The Mark Mason ceremony of Acknowledgement will be performed.
The Mark Masons Lodge will be closed.
A Craft Lodge will be declared open in the 3rd degree.
A Mark Master Masons Lodge will be opened.
The ceremony of Advancement will be performed.
The Mark Master Masons Lodge will be closed.
A Craft Lodge will be declared closed in the 3rd and 2nd degrees.
A Craft Lodge will be closed in the 1st degree.

Narrator

Brethren, we give you a most cordial welcome and we hope that you will get both interest and entertainment from these scenes from the past.

During the evening you will hear phrases and words with which you may be familiar in other degrees today. Please do not say to yourself that this is from the Craft, or the Royal Arch, or one of the Allied degrees. Remember rather that you are seeing the evidence for saying that the original Mark degree was, in its many varied forms, nearly as old as the Craft ceremonies themselves. After the Union of 1813 and the severance of the Craft (with the Royal Arch) from other forms of Freemasonry it is hardly surprising that various portions of the older Mark workings should have been adopted by other degrees, especially those that had a more recent origin.

You are requested to remain seated throughout the proceedings as the instructions are directed to the team alone.

Brethren, we now go backwards in time, to the period between 1780 and 1850 and you are to witness the ceremony of Acknowledgement in a Mark Mason (or Mark Man) lodge.

Before I ask our Master to open his Lodge it is necessary for me to mention the subject of dreams. The V. S. L. tells us that Joseph having (by means of false evidence) been cast into prison for refusing to commit adultery with the wife of his employer (Potiphar), was able to interpret the dreams of two other prisoners – the one-time baker and the one-time butler of the Pharaoh. The Baker was to be hanged and the Butler restored to favour. Both interpretations

Mark Mason wearing an early 19th-century 'keystone style' apron of Albany Lodge, No. 176, Newport, Isle of Wight.

proved correct, as chapters 39–41 of the Book of Genesis tell us. The Butler, remembering the incident, recommended Joseph to Pharaoh when the latter was also troubled by the dream of the seven fat and the seven lean kine. Joseph interpreted this dream correctly and afterwards occupied a very important position in Egypt.

Many hundreds of years later Nebuchadnezzar was troubled by a dream which Daniel interpreted for him, and Daniel afterwards became a very distinguished figure among the Persians.

Compared with the task of Daniel, Joseph had a very simple one to perform. Pharaoh told Joseph the facts of his dream, whereas Nebuchadnezzar refused to give any particulars whatsoever and demanded of Daniel both what he had dreamed and the interpretation of it. Our ancient brethren transferred the whole of the latter event to the reign of a later king of Persia (probably Darius) and made their ritual fit this arrangement.

(Pause whilst Preceptor opens V.S.L. and turns second degree Tracing Board face upwards)

Worshipful Master, will you please open a Mark Masons Lodge.

Worshipful Master

(Gavels)

Before opening a Mark Masons Lodge I duly declare that a Craft Lodge has already been opened in the first and second degrees.
(Pause whilst Junior Deacon and Candidate stand in North-West)
I duly enquire of the Candidate: Brother [name], have you petitioned that you might receive the promise of a Mark Mason?

Candidate

(prompted by Junior Deacon and with F.C. sign)

I have, Worshipful Master.

Worshipful Master

Then it is necessary that you should prove yourself to be possessed of the five senses of mankind, for which purpose the Junior Deacon will conduct you round the Lodge.

(Junior Deacon leads the Candidate to the Master's pedestal on which lies a scroll of vellum or parchment)

Worshipful Master

(Gavels)

Brother [name], you will unroll the scroll of vellum or parchment which lies before you and communicate to us its contents.
(Candidate unrolls the scroll and reads aloud the contents)

Worshipful Master

(Gavels)

Brethren, our Brother is possessed of the senses of hearing and seeing.
(Junior Deacon leads the Candidate to the Junior Warden who places a phial underneath the nose of the Candidate)

Junior Warden

Brother [name], what is that?

Candidate

Frankincense.

Junior Warden

(Gavels)

Our Brother is possessed of the sense of smell.
(Junior Deacon leads the Candidate to the Senior Warden where he is invited to taste a substance)

Senior Warden

Brother [name], what is that?

Candidate

Manna, and it is good.

Junior Warden
(Gavels)

Our Brother is possessed of the sense of taste.
(Junior Deacon leads Candidate to the Inner Guard who applies the large compasses, extended at 90 degrees, with points to breast and navel)

Candidate
(reacts visibly)

Inner Guard
(with F.C. sign)

Our Brother is possessed of the sense of feeling.

Worshipful Master
(to Candidate)

Brother {name}, you will now retire for preparation.
(Both Junior Deacon and Candidate retire, Senior Deacon retires and Junior Deacon re-enters the Lodge. Senior Deacon puts on a white Sojourner's surplice – outside the door)

(The Master and Wardens put on robes denoting their regal and gubernatorial functions {red and purple only} and the King has a sceptre. The King sits on his usual 'throne' and adopts a reclining posture)

(Junior Deacon places a cable-tow round the Candidate's chest, places ladder on the floor between the Junior Warden and the Senior Warden, turns T.B. face downwards, and covers V.S.L. with a veil)

(Preceptor extinguishes candles)

Narrator

Brethren, the scene is set as in the audience chamber of a King of Persia. The ladder between the Wardens' pedestals represents a pontoon bridge across the River Euphrates. The V.S.L. is covered with a veil as the scriptures could have no possible place in a Persian palace.

The Candidate enters as a Fellowcraft without apron, and no salutes are given. He is symbolically 'in bondage' and his bonds today are represented by the cable-tow placed around his chest. In some lodges he actually wore leg-irons and manacles. The position of the cable-tow showed his progress, for in the E.A. degree it was around his throat and in the third degree around his waist. These positions were then referred to as the Gutteral, the Pectoral, and the Umbilical.

It is to be presumed that as the King does not speak Hebrew and the Candidate does not speak Persian the Sojourner acts as the interpreter and answers throughout.

Worshipful Master

(Gavels)

Brethren, assist me to open a Mark Masons Lodge.
Brother Junior Warden, what is the first care of every Mark Mason?

Junior Warden

(with F.C. sign)

To prove the Lodge close tyled.

Worshipful Master

Direct that duty to be done.

Junior Warden

Brother Inner Guard, you will prove the Lodge close tyled.

Inner Guard

(gives F.C. knocks)

Tyler

(gives F.C. knocks)

Inner Guard

(with F.C. sign)

Brother Junior Warden, the Lodge proves close tyled.

Junior Warden

(gives one knock and with F.C. sign)
Worshipful master, the Lodge is close tyled.

Worshipful Master

Brother Senior Warden, what is the next care?

Senior Warden

(with F.C. sign)

To see that the Brethren stand to order as Fellowcrafts.

Worshipful Master

To order, Brethren, as Fellowcraft Freemasons.
I declare this to be a Mark Masons Lodge for the purpose of acknowledging Brother [name].

(Discharges F.C. sign and gives Mark Master Mason knocks – Team also discharge F.C. sign)

(Senior Warden, Junior Warden, Inner Guard, and Tyler all give Mark Master Mason knocks in turn)

(All give Penal sign i.e. left hand chopping off right hand, which is done by holding hand out horizontally with the Mark Man sign manual and then rubbing vertical left hand edge over wrist.)

Worshipful Master

Brethren, be seated.

CEREMONY

Tyler

(gives Mark Master Mason knocks)

Inner Guard

(opens door and stands in doorway)

Who comes here?

Tyler

A Sojourner seeks admission.

Inner Guard

Wait while I report him to the King.

(closes door, proceeds via North-West, steps forward with Grand and Royal sign and then discharges it before speaking)

O King, a Sojourner seeks admission.

King

Admit him.
(Sojourner is admitted by Inner Guard, proceeds via the North-West, steps forward with Grand and Royal sign and then discharges it before speaking)

Sojourner

O King, live for ever! We have been in search throughout all thy dominions, amongst the magicians, the astrologers and soothsayers, but we can find no one who can tell thee thy dreams or give thee interpretation thereof.

King

Go, search again.
(Sojourner withdraws)

Narrator

Persia, being a very large country, a considerable time is now supposed to have elapsed.

Tyler
(gives Mark Master Mason knocks)

Inner Guard
(opens door and stands in doorway)
Who comes here?

Tyler

The Sojourner seeks readmission.

Inner Guard

Wait while I report to the King.
(closes door, proceeds via North-West, steps forward with Grand and Royal sign and then discharges it before speaking)
O King, the Sojourner seeks readmission.

King

Let him be readmitted.
(Inner Guard opens the door for the Sojourner and the Candidate, who enter and proceed via North-West, Sojourner steps forward with Grand and Royal sign and then discharges it before speaking)

Sojourner

O King, live for ever! We have again been in search throughout all your dominions, amongst the magicians, the astrologers and the soothsayers and have found one, a captive of the tribe of Judah, who can tell thee thy dream, and give thee an interpretation thereof.

King

What is his Name?

Narrator

His name is the same as the Craft Installed Master's word which is used today.

King

The man that can tell me my dream and give me the interpretation thereof shall be clothed in purple and scarlet, shall be sat upon mine own horse and proclaimed before me as the Third Person in my kingdom.

Sojourner

(with Grand and Royal sign)

O King, live for ever! The dream is not from me, but from him who sent me. Thou dreamest that thou sawest a great lion standing at thy bedside ready to devour thee and thy household.

King

That is indeed my dream. Give me now the interpretation thereof.

Sojourner

(with Grand and Royal sign)

O King, the great lion that thou sawest by thy bedside was the Lion of the Tribe of Judah, ready to devour thee and thy household if thou will not let this captive go down to Jerusalem, there to receive the promise of a Mark Man.

King

Loose him from his bonds, clothe him in purple and scarlet, sit him upon my horse, and proclaim him before me as the Third Person in my kingdom.

Early Mark tracing board of the Star in the East Lodge, No. 95, Scarborough.

Sojourner

(with Grand and Royal sign)

O King, that is not my request.

King

What is thy request?

Sojourner

(with Grand and Royal sign)

That thou wouldst pass this man down to Tatnai, Governor on this side of the river, Tatnai to pass him over to Shethar Boznai and his companions on the other side of the river, and Shethar Boznai to pass him down to Jerusalem, there to receive the promise of a Mark Mason, and to have Corn, Wine, Oil and Salt for his sustenance while he assists in rebuilding the Temple and Holy City which now be in ruins, and do all that his forefathers have done before him.

King

Most willingly I grant thy request; and whatsoever shall alter this decree shall have the timber pulled from off his house, set up as a gallows, himself hanged therefrom, and his house made a dunghill for ever.
(the Candidate is loosed from his bonds by the Sojourner and led {i.e. Sojourner Proceeds, followed by Candidate} to the Junior Warden who represents Tatnai.)

Sojourner

O Tatnai, Governor, it is the King's decree that you pass this man over to Shethar Boznai.

Junior Warden

According to the King's decree I pass this man over to Shethar Boznai and his companions.
(the Candidate, preceded by the Sojourner, crosses the bridge to South side of the Senior Warden who represents Shethar Boznai)

Sojourner

O Shethar Boznai, it is the King's decree that you pass this man down to Jerusalem, there to receive the promise of a Mark Mason, and to have Corn, Wine, Oil, and Salt for his sustenance while he assists in the rebuilding of the Temple and Holy City which now be in ruins, and do all that his forefathers have done before him.

Senior Warden

According to the King's decree I pass this man down to Jerusalem, there to receive the promise of a Mark Mason.
(Sojourner withdraws with Candidate following)
(Junior Deacon removes ladder and unveils V.S.L., Wardens take off their gubernatorial robes. Inner Guard puts on the surplice of Scribe N. {Preceptor relights candles}. Tracing Board remains face downwards)

Narrator

Brethren, the scene has changed and you are now to imagine yourselves in the Audience chamber of Zerubbabel, Prince of the People.

Tyler
(gives Mark Master Mason knocks)

Scribe N.
(with Grand and Royal sign)

Most Excellent, there is an alarm.

Most Excellent Zerubbabel

Attend to it.

Scribe N.
(opens door)

Whom have you there?

Tyler

A captive of the Tribe of Judah, who, having been released from his Babylonish captivity and having traversed through great dangers and difficulties, has come to offer his services towards that great and glorious undertaking, the rebuilding of the Holy Temple to God's service.

Scribe N.

Wait while I report to the Most Excellent.
(closes door, proceeds to North-West, gives Grand and Royal sign)
Most Excellent, a captive of the Tribe of Judah, who, having been released from his Babylonish captivity and having traversed through great dangers and difficulties, has come to offer his services towards that great and glorious undertaking, the rebuilding of the Holy Temple to God's service.

Most Excellent Zerubbabel

What is his name?

Narrator

His name is that of an Installed Master in the Craft.

Most Excellent Zerubbabel

What is he?

Scribe N.
(with Grand and Royal sign)

A stone-squarer.

Most Excellent Zerubbabel

As it is the hope of reward that at all times sweetens labour, what is his desire?

Scribe N.
(with Grand and Royal sign)

Acknowledgment as a Mark Mason.

Most Excellent Zerubbabel

Does he bring an example of his work?

Scribe N.
(with Grand and Royal sign)

He does.

Most Excellent Zerubbabel

Then let him be admitted.
(Scribe N. opens the door for the Candidate, who enters with Rough Ashlar, advances directly to the East followed by the Sojourner, stands in front of Most Excellent Zerubbabel's pedestal and hands him the Ashlar.)

Most Excellent Zerubbabel
(examines the stone)

Know ye not that no stone can be used for the rebuilding of the Holy Temple unless it is polished in all its surfaces and is true die square? Your work is rejected and will be heaved over amongst the rubble.
(hands the stone back to the candidate)

Candidate

(prompted by the Sojourner)
Most Excellent, I was not aware of the requirements of the builders, but if permitted to do so I will proceed to the quarries and there prepare a stone such as you desire and describe.

Most Excellent Zerubbabel

As you have traversed through great dangers and difficulties in order to offer your services in our great and glorious undertaking I am loath to say you nay. I therefore permit you to proceed to the quarries, that you may there prepare other and better evidence of your ability.
(Candidate withdraws followed by the Sojourner

Pause for up to a minute.

Tyler
(gives Mark Master Mason knocks)

Scribe N.
(with Grand and Royal sign)

Most Excellent, there is an alarm.

Most Excellent Zerubbabel

Attend to it.

Scribe N.
(opens door)

Whom have you there?

Tyler

The released captive from Babylon who was permitted to proceed to the quarries, there to prepare other work, seeks admission so that he may submit his work for inspection.

Scribe N.

Wait while I report to the Most Excellent.
(closes door, goes to North-West, gives Grand and Royal sign)
Most Excellent, the released captive from Babylon, whom you permitted to

proceed to the quarries, there to prepare other and better evidence of his ability, now seeks admission so that he may submit his work for your inspection.

Most Excellent Zerubbabel

Admit him.
(Scribe N. opens door to admit the Candidate, who enters followed by the Sojourner, proceeds direct to West and, standing in front of Most Excellent Zerubbabel's pedestal, hands him the polished Ashlar for inspection.)

Most Excellent Zerubbabel

(uses try-square on the Ashlar but does not test it with the maul)

I acknowledge the ability displayed in the execution of your work. It is approved and shall be passed on to the Builders.
Go, choose your Mark, and place it upon the Sacred Writings.
(Candidate is conducted by the Sojourner to the Secretary's table where he chooses a Mark. Both remain there whilst:

- *The Master (Most Excellent Zerubbabel), Sojourner, and Inner Guard remove their robes;*
- *the Junior Deacon turns the Tracing Board face upwards, and places kneeling stool at West of central pedestal;*
- *The Sojourner (who is now the Senior Deacon) conducts the Candidate to the West side of the central pedestal.*
- *The candidate places his Mark upon the V.S.L.)*

Narrator

Brethren, we are again assembled in a Fellow Crafts Lodge.

(Master gives one knock. All rise. Master proceeds to the East side of the central pedestal)

Worshipful Master

You will kneel as a Fellowcraft.

(Candidate kneels on right knee with his left foot forming a square)
Place your right hand on the V.S.L., and repeat the following obligation.
(All give Sign of Fidelity at the same time as the Master)

[Obligation of a Mark Mason now follows]

Candidate
(repeats after the Master)

I [name],
/ in the name of the Great Overseer of the Square /
/ and of this Worthy and Worshipful Lodge of Mark Masons /
/ duly constituted /
/ regularly assembled /
/ and properly dedicated to His service /
/ do hereby and hereon /
/ most solemnly promise and swear /
/ that I will not be /
/ at the making of a Brother Mark Mason /
/ unless there be /
/ 3 – 5 – 7 – 9 or 11 Brother Mark Masons present /
/ and that I will not be /
/ at the making of a Brother Mark Mason /
/ of an inferior degree in Masonry /
/ to the one I have received myself. /
/ I furthermore do promise /
/ vow /
/ and swear /
/ that I will not be /
/ at the making of a Brother Mark Mason /
/ unless he pays one half Shekel for his Mark /
/ and that I will not send /
/ this my Mark /
/ to a Brother Mark Mason /
/ except I be in want or necessity /
/ and not *that* a second time /
/ except the former be redeemed. /
/ To all these several points /

/ I swear /
/ under no less a penalty /
/ than that of having /
/ my R...H...S...A...T...W...A...S...O...M...L...B...T...T...W...D...
(right hand severed at the wrist and slung over my left breast there to wither and decay)

Worshipful Master

In order to render this, which is but a serious promise, a solemn obligation, binding on you so long as you shall live, I call on you to salute the Holy Word with your lips.
Arise, duly obligated Brother Mark Mason.
(All sit)
I am now permitted to explain to you your Mark.

Narrator

This was done in the Worshipful Master's own particular words, and not as a part of the ritual.

Worshipful Master

I may also add that should you be reduced by real want or necessity, on presenting your Mark to a Brother Mark Mason, explaining your circumstances, he will be bound to relieve you to the extent of one half a Shekel *(Author's Note: which is equivalent to approximately five pence in today's currency)* but you are bound to return it as soon as you are able.

Brother [name], you will now listen to various lectures which expound the history and origin of this Degree.

(Worshipful Master returns to his pedestal in the East.)

(Senior Deacon conducts the Candidate to the North-West)

Historical Part

(Delivered from the South-East)

At the building of King Solomon's Temple, there were a great many workmen employed; they consisted of Entered Apprentices and Fellowcrafts.

The Entered Apprentices received a weekly supply of corn, wine, oil, and salt, but the Fellowcrafts got theirs in specie, which they received in the Middle Chamber of King Solomon's Temple. The stones for the Temple were cut and wrought in the quarries of Judea, and there carved, marked, and numbered. To each Fellowcraft our Grand Master Hiram gave a mark, so that when the stones came down to the Temple, they fitted their place according to their Mark. The entered Apprentices seeing this, put marks on their stones to obtain the wages of Fellowcrafts. Hiram, finding his money come short, could not tell where his deficiency lay, unless it was among the Entered Apprentices, so he built a place on purpose to pay the Fellowcrafts their wages and ordered them to bring Marks in their hands in this position

(Mark Man position)

and put them through a hole in the door. They showed their Marks. They had their money given them and went away satisfied. The Entered Apprentices observing this put their hands through likewise, but when they opened them they showed no Mark. So a man was stationed behind the door with a drawn sword, ready to cut off the hands of those in which there were no Marks. Those who escaped went away ashamed, rubbing across the wrists their right hands in this form

(last part of the present sign)

which has since been used as the sign of a Mark Mason. When the stones on which there were fictitious Marks were brought down to the Temple, they would not fit their places according to their mark, so men were stationed at the top of the building with their hands in this form *(the present second sign)* and a word was given *Ekbetain* and means 'heave over'. They heaved them over, and from the immense height the stones had to fall, they became the rubble in which our Grand Master was first interred.

The Charge

(Delivered from the South-East)

Brother [name], allow me to congratulate you on being thought worthy to be promoted to the honourable degree of a Mark Mason.

Permit me to impress on your mind that your assiduity should ever be commensurate with your duties, which become more and more extensive as you advance in Masonry.

The situation to which you are now promoted will not only draw upon you the scrutinising eyes of the world, but also those of your Brethren on whom this degree has not been conferred.

All are justified in expecting that your conduct may be such as can with safety be imitated, but in the honourable capacity of a Mark Mason, it is more especially expected that your conduct in the Lodge, and among your fellows, should be such as to stand the test of the Great Overseer of the Square, and not like the work of the negligent and unfaithful of former times, to be rejected and thrown aside as unfit for the spiritual building eternal in the heavens.

For I would remind you that the stone which the builders rejected, because possessing virtues to them unknown, became the Head of the Corner.

Narrator

In the course of the questions that follow the grip is the present day Pass-Grip with the thumbs lying flat. The word is *kebrioth* pronounced 'kay-bay-ree-oath' which literally means 'Friends of the letter' or 'Companions of the Mark'.

The sign is the last part of the present day penal sign accompanied by a rubbing motion with the edge of the left hand across the wrist.

Questions before Closing

(Questioner stands in the South-East. Answerer stands in the North-West next to the candidate, both facing East)

Q.

Brother [name] are you a Mark Mason?

A.

I am.

Q.

How came you to be a Mark Mason?

A.

Being one of the Captives of the Tribe of Judah I was bound hand and foot and brought before the King of Babylon.

Q.

Why were you brought before the King?

A.

The King, having dreamed a dream which all the magicians, the astrologers and soothsayers could not interpret, I prayed to the God of Heaven who made the matter known to the King, for which he released me from my bondage and passed me down to Tatnai, Governor of this side of the river, Tatnai passed me over to Shethar Boznai and his companions on the other side of the river, who passed me down to Jerusalem, there to receive the promise of a Mark Man.

Q.

What is the promise of a Mark Mason?

A.

That I should keep the secrets of a Mark Mason from all those who are not found worthy.

Q.

What are the secrets of a Mark Mason?

A.

A grip, word, and sign.

Q.

Advance to me as a Mark Mason and give the secrets.

(both Questioner and Answerer advance to the centre, the sign, grip and word are communicated after which the Questioner and Answerer return to their former places)

Q.

What further privileges have you as a Mark Mason?

A.

That all Mark Masons should wear, in the fifth buttonhole on that part of the garment called vest or waistcoat, a white ribbon with a pendant or medal hanging thereto.

Q.

Why in my fifth buttonhole?

A.

Because there are five senses in man.

Q.

Which I will thank you to name?

A.

Hearing, Seeing, Smelling, Tasting, and Feeling.

Q.

What other Decree did the King make?

A.

That whoever should alter his Decree should have the timber pulled from his house, set up as a gallows, himself hanged therefrom and his house made a dunghill forever.

Q.

Who sought to alter the King's Decree?

A.

Haaman (pronounced Hay-a-man), the Jew's enemy.

Q.

What became of Haaman?

A.

The timber was pulled from his house, set up as a gallows, himself hanged **thereon.**
(Senior Deacon conducts the Candidate to a seat in the Lodge and then resumes his own)

Closing a Mark Masons Lodge

Worshipful Master

(gavels once)

To order, Brethren, as Mark Masons.
(The Brethren stand to order with the last part of the present Penal sign)

Worshipful Master

I declare this Mark Masons lodge closed.
(The Brethren complete the sign with the rubbing motion)
(The Worshipful Master, Senior Warden, Junior Warden, Inner Guard, and Tyler all knock. All sit)

Narrator

Brethren, that concludes the Ceremony of Acknowledgement in a Mark Masons Lodge in the period 1780 to 1850.
The Worshipful Master will shortly open a Mark Master Mason's Lodge of about 1850 working.

(Instructions to Team alone)

(After the opening of the Mark Master Mason lodge the Fellowcraft Tracing Board will be removed, revealing the Third Degree Tracing Board.

The Square and Compasses on the V.S.L. will be adjusted to the third degree position).

Part 2: The Mark Master Degree Ceremony

Revised 12 January 1987

Instructions To Demonstration Team

The Master and Wardens are in their present positions but there is no wicket at the Senior Warden's pedestal. The Worshipful Master's pedestal is described below. The Overseers sit in the centre of the lodge, relative to each other as today, but facing inwards and with a considerable space between them. This is necessary as the main pedestal is in the centre of the lodge with the V.S.L. and the square and compasses open upon it in the 3rd Degree position. This pedestal is surrounded by the three lesser lights placed in an equilateral triangle position with the apex to the East. The kneeling stool is placed between the base lights.

The Tracing Board is placed between the kneeling stool and the Senior Warden's pedestal, allowing room for the floorwork. The distance between the kneeling stool and the Tracing Board must be sufficient to allow the four gliding steps to be taken.

The Inspector sits on the right of the Worshipful Master and Narrator on his left. The Secretary is called the Registrar and sits in the North.

All members of the team wear Craft aprons. With the exception of the Master, the Inspector, and the Narrator who wear Past Master's aprons, and the Candidate who wears a F.C. apron, the team wear Master Mason's aprons. Six Brethren in the North and six in the South will take part in the opening and closing processions; these brethren will also wear Master Mason's aprons.

In opening this demonstration lodge the method of standing to order is to place the hands on the hips, thumbs pointing *backwards*. The word is *adoniram* (pronounced 'a-DON-i-RAM', with the emphases on the 2nd and 4th syllables).

The Grand Sign is given by one brother extending his right hand (in a horizontal position, palm downwards) with the first and second fingers extended and separated. The third and fourth fingers are closed into the palm of the hand and covered by the thumb. The sign is completed by the responding brother placing the first and second fingers of his LEFT hand, likewise extended, across the fingers of the questioning brother, thus forming a simple 'lattice'.

Narrator

The ritual and ceremony we are now to witness is composed from three old rituals combining, we hope, the best of each. The extracts used are strictly accurate but in certain places the original is so long-winded that a précis of salient features is described.

As no old ritual mentions any sign to be used when addressing a superior officer we shall use the sign of Fidelity to preserve the dignity of the proceedings.

One thing more: the Grand Sign is known as the 'Crossed Fingers' or 'Lines of Parallel' and when complete represents the lattice framework of the Mark Cipher which will be explained during the ceremony.

(Grand Sign is here demonstrated by the two preceptors)

In these old rituals the Junior Warden had to test every brother present with this sign but today, to again save time, we are asking the Junior Warden to test only the Overseers and then to communicate the sign and word to the Senior Warden who will pass them on to the Master.

Worshipful Master, I now request you to open a lodge of Mark Masters.

Opening a Lodge of Mark Master Masons

Worshipful Master

(Gavels)

Brethren, assist me to open a lodge of Mark Masters.
(all Rise)

Worshipful Master

Brother Junior Warden, what is the first care of a Mark Master?

Junior Warden

To see the lodge properly tyled.

Worshipful Master

Direct that duty to be done.

Junior Warden

Brother Inner Guard, see the lodge properly tyled.
(Inner Guard knocks, Tyler knocks)

Inner Guard

Brother Junior Warden, the lodge is properly tyled.

Junior Warden

Worshipful Master, the lodge is properly tyled.

Worshipful Master

Brother Senior Warden, what is the next care?

Senior Warden

To see that none but Mark Masters are present.

Worshipful Master

To order, brethren, as Mark Masters.
(Brethren stand to order with hands on hips, thumbs behind)

Worshipful Master

Brother Junior Warden, are you a Mark Master?

Junior Warden

I am, Worshipful Master, try me and prove me.

Worshipful Master

By what test will you be proved?

Junior Warden

By the knowledge of that stone hewn by no mortal hands, which was rejected by the builders, but afterwards became the head of the corner.

Worshipful Master

Being yourself so well acquainted with the proper mode you will prove the brethren present Mark Master Masons by signs and demonstrate the same to me by copying their example.
(Junior Warden drops sign, leaves his pedestal and, proceeding clockwise, tests the Overseers with the Grand sign and reports to the Senior Warden)

Junior Warden

(in front of the Senior Warden's pedestal)
Brother Senior Warden, the brethren are all Mark Masters.

Senior Warden

Brother Junior Warden, you will give me the proof.
(Junior Warden goes to left of Senior Warden's pedestal, gives him the sign and word secretly, returns to his seat and resumes hands on hips)

Senior Warden

Worshipful Master, I confirm that all the Brethren are Mark Masters.

Worshipful Master

Brother Junior Warden, your office in the lodge?

Junior Warden

To examine the mark of every brother and, if correct, to pass them to the Senior Warden to receive their wages.

Worshipful Master

Brother Senior Warden, what are the duties of your office?

Senior Warden

To examine the work performed by every craftsman, compare it with his mark and to give to each the reward of his labour.

Worshipful Master

Brother Senior Warden , the situation of the Master?

Senior Warden

In the East and as the representative of Adoniram to preside over the brethren at their labours.

Worshipful Master

I acknowledge you all to be Mark Masters and I now declare this lodge open *(all discharge sign)* for the purpose of receiving reports from our Inspector and any advancing Craftsmen.

Wherefore, brethren, lay aside all malice and guile and hypocrisies, and envies and all evil speakings, if so be that ye have tasted that the Lord is gracious. Unto whom coming, as unto a living stone, disallowed indeed of men, but chosen of God and precious, ye also as living stones are to be built up into a spiritual house, an holy priesthood, to offer sacrifices acceptable unto God.

Brethren, this is the will of God, that with well doing ye put to silence the ignorance of foolish men. As free, but not using your liberty as a cloak of maliciousness, but as servants of God.

Honour all men, Love the brotherhood, Fear God, Honour the King.

Brethren, in the name and fear of the Grand Omnipotent I declare this lodge opened for the purpose of Mark Master Masonry.

(Worshipful Master, Senior Warden, Junior Warden, Inner Guard and Tyler all knock)

(All sit except Deacons and candidate, who retire to the Tyler's room for preparation)

Narrator

We now proceed immediately to the Ceremony of Advancement.
In the Tyler's room the Deacons have satisfied themselves that the candidate is proficient in the three Craft degrees and that he is a Mark Mason, including the inspection of his Mark there given. The Senior Deacon then addresses him thus:

Senior Deacon

You represent a skilled craftsman seeking to be advanced to that higher class of workmen to whom, at the building of the Temple, the superintendence of the materials and work was entrusted. You must, therefore, present yourself free of cumbersome apparel, ready for work and provided with a specimen of your masterpiece.

Narrator

The candidate is then divested of his coat, collar and tie, or waistcoat if he wears one. He rolls up his sleeves, dons a stone worker's apron and is handed a Keystone. The Deacons also don stone workers' aprons.
(Candidate gives the knocks of a Fellowcraft)

Inner Guard

(opens door)

Whom have you there?

Senior Deacon

Brother [name], a candidate for advancement.

Inner Guard

Has he the password?

Senior Deacon

He has not, I will give it for him.
(Whispers 'Joppa')

Inner Guard

Halt while I report to the Master.
(Closes door)
(With sign of fidelity)

Worshipful Master

Brother [name], a candidate for Advancement under the password 'Joppa'.

Worshipful Master

Admit him.
(Inner Guard opens door and admits Junior Deacon, Senior Deacon, and Candidate, in that order, who stand in the West facing the Worshipful Master, Senior Deacon in centre, Junior Deacon on his right, Candidate on his left. Junior Deacon carries a cube stone, and Candidate his keystone)

Senior Deacon

(Takes keystone from Candidate)
Salute the Worshipful Master as a Fellowcraft then as a Master Mason.
(Candidate does so. Senior Deacon returns keystone to him)

Worshipful Master

Let the Craftsmen present their masterpieces to the Overseers who will report to the Senior Warden their qualifications for Advancement.
(Junior Deacon, Senior Deacon & Candidate, in that order, proceed to the Junior

Overseer's Pedestal where they halt and face Junior Deacon. Senior Deacon taps Junior Overseer on the right shoulder four times)

Junior Overseer

Whom have you there?

Senior Deacon

Craftsmen with their masterpieces for your approval.

Junior Overseer

I will examine them with pleasure.
(Junior Deacon presents his cube stone. Junior Overseer strikes stone once with his gavel and tries it with his square)

Junior Overseer

Pass, your work is approved.
(Returns stone to Junior Deacon)
(Candidate, instructed by Senior Deacon, presents his Keystone to Junior Overseer who looks at it only)

Junior Overseer

The form of this stone is unusual. *(Hands it back to Candidate)*. I cannot pass it without the concurrence of my Brother Overseers. Brother Senior Overseer, may I call your attention to this Brother's masterpiece.
(Deacons, in same order as before, conduct the candidate to the Senior Overseer's pedestal and stand facing the Senior Overseer)
(Senior Deacon taps S.O. on the right shoulder four times)

Senior Overseer

Whom have you there?

Senior Deacon

Craftsmen with their masterpieces for your approval.

Senior Overseer

I will examine them with pleasure.
(Junior Deacon presents his cube stone. Senior Overseer strikes it once with his gavel and tries it with his square)

Senior Overseer

Your work is approved.
(Hands stone back to Junior Deacon)
(Candidate, instructed by Senior Deacon, presents his Keystone to Senior Overseer who looks at it only)

Senior Overseer

This is indeed a curiously wrought stone.
(Hands stone back to Candidate)
We must consult the Master Overseer. Brother Master Overseer, will you oblige us with your opinion of this stone?
(Deacons, in same order as before, conduct candidate to the Master Overseer's pedestal and stand facing Master Overseer)
(Senior Deacon taps Master Overseer on the right shoulder four times)

Master Overseer

Whom have you there?

Senior Deacon

Craftsmen with their masterpieces for your approval.

Master Overseer

I will examine them with pleasure.
(Junior Deacon presents his cube stone. Master Overseer strikes it once with his gavel and tries it with his square)

Master Overseer

Pass, your work is approved and will be passed to the builders. Give this

certificate to the Senior Warden and you will receive your wages.
(Master Overseer places the stone at the left of his pedestal)
(Candidate, instructed by Senior Deacon, presents his Keystone. Master Overseer looks at it)

Master Overseer

(To Deacons and Candidate)

Stand aside.
(Deacons and Candidate move to the right of the Master Overseer and stand a foot or so away, facing him)

Master Overseer

Brother Overseers, you have asked for my opinion of this stone. Approach and let us examine it together.
(Senior Overseer and Junior Overseer leave their seats and stand one upon either side of the Master Overseer. They confer together for about half a minute. Master Overseer rises)

Master Overseer

My Brethren, I cannot perceive the use to which such a stone could be applied.
(Turns to Candidate)
For what use is it intended?

Candidate

(Prompted by Senior Deacon)

This is a stone which I found on my way hither.

Senior Deacon

(Candidate does not repeat)

These characters are *(Points to them but is hastily interrupted by)*...

Master Overseer

...not the work of any of our Craft. This stone was not even made by you.
(Master Overseer looks enquiringly towards the Senior Overseer and Junior Overseer who give the heave-over sign, which is to throw the right hand upwards and outwards)

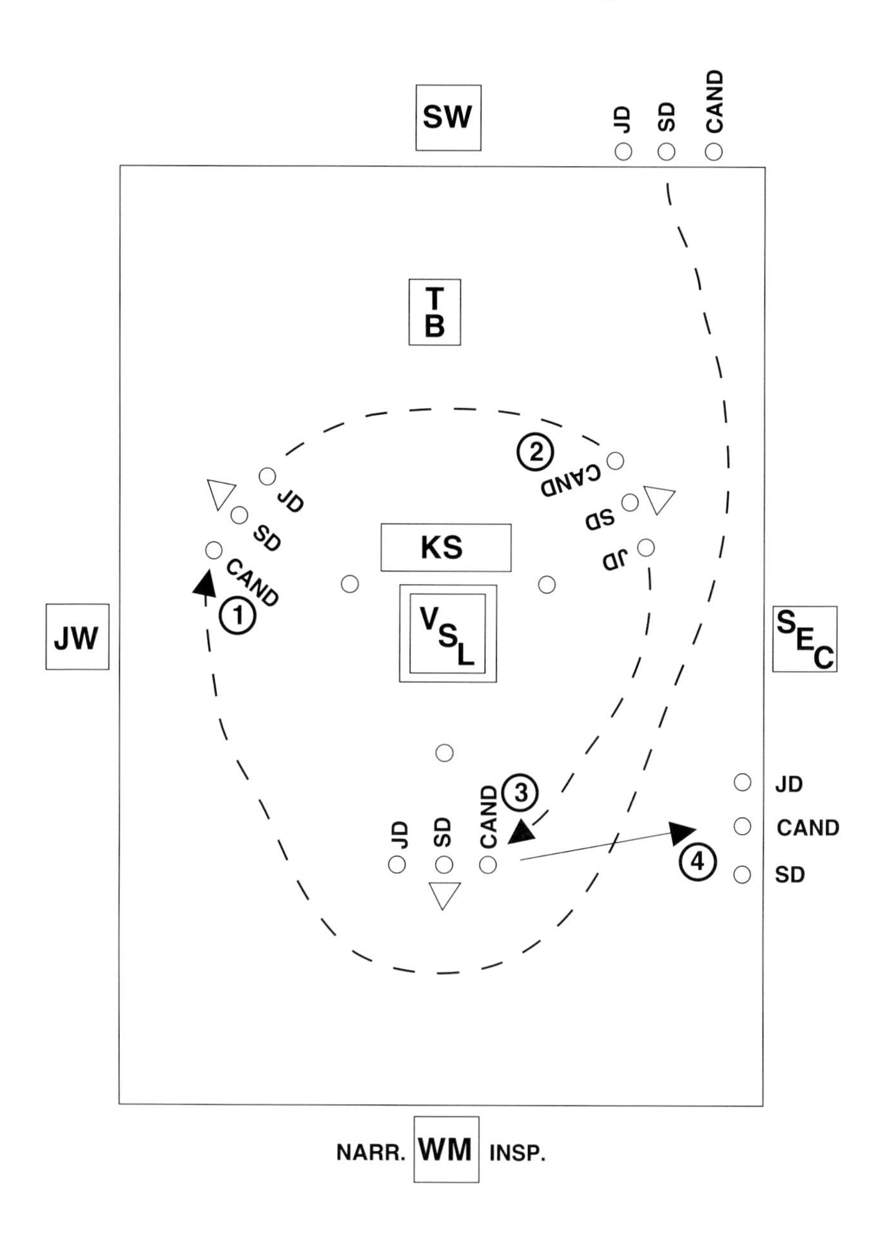

Refers to ritual on page 88.

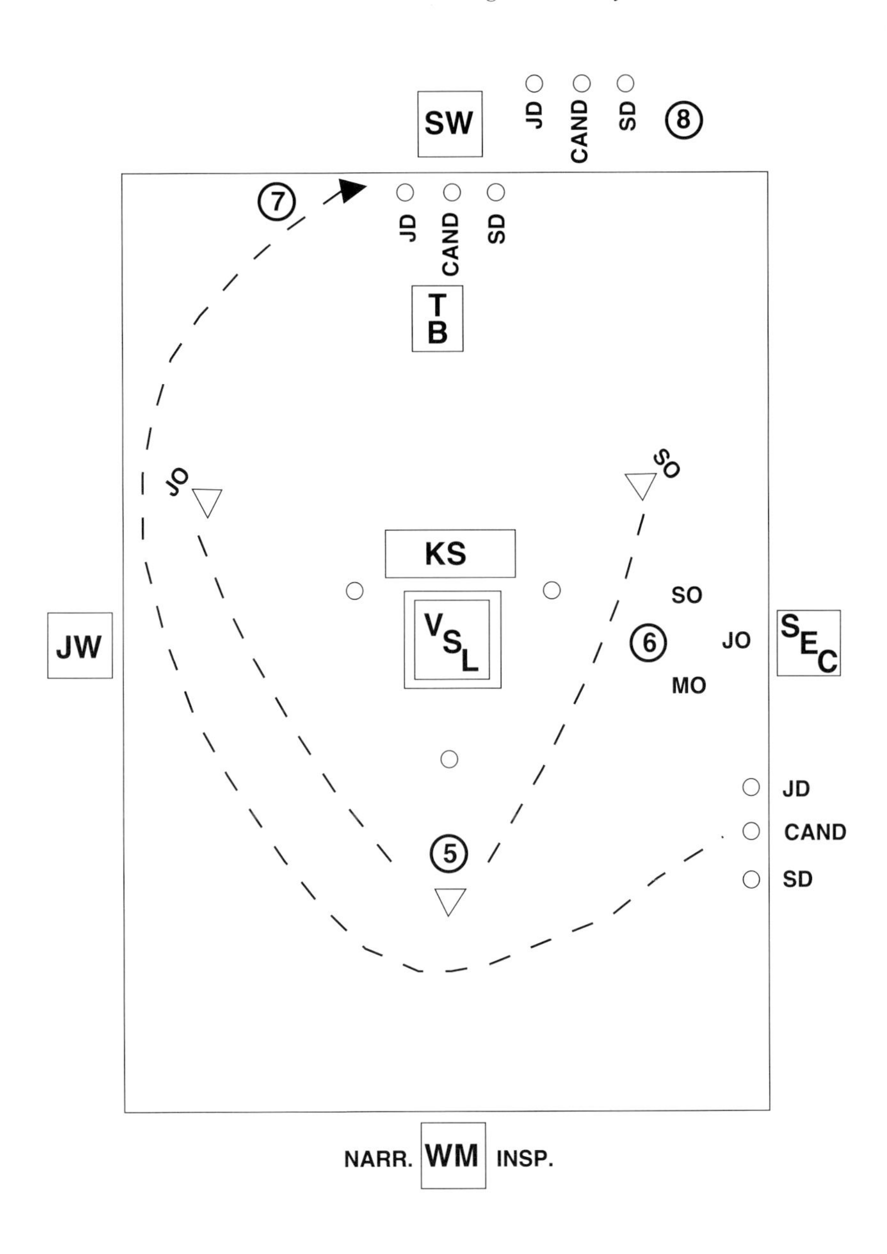

Refers to ritual on page 88.

Master Overseer

It is obviously unfit for any building. We reject it.
(All three Overseers move to the North.)
(The Master Overseer and Senior Overseer heave it over with a similar movement to today save that it is caught by the Junior Overseer who deposits it in the North, half hidden beneath the secretary's table and so placed as to be easily kicked by a passing foot)
(The Overseers resume their places)

Master Overseer
(Addressing Candidate sternly)

Go! Your conduct is indefensible.
(Senior Deacon, Candidate, and Junior Deacon move, in that order, behind the Master Overseer and Junior Overseer chairs and stand facing Senior Warden. Junior Deacon hands his certificate to Senior Warden who gives him a coin, Candidate then presents his hand as a Mark Mason to Senior Warden who seizes it)

Senior Warden

Hold, you betray yourself. Brother Master Overseer, who is this man?

Master Overseer
(Rising, with sign of fidelity)

One whose work has been rejected.

Senior Warden

Then seize and detain him.
(The Deacons do so and march Candidate directly to left of Senior Warden and turn about to face East with Candidate in centre, Junior Deacon on his right, Senior Deacon on his left. All three must stand well back, slightly behind Senior Warden)

Senior Warden
(Takes Junior Deacon's hand and with sign of fidelity addresses Worshipful Master)

Worshipful Sir, I present this candidate for advancement.

Worshipful Master

I congratulate you upon your success and will now ask the Senior Warden to invest you with the jewel.

Senior Warden

(Invests Candidate with jewel)

Brother [name], by command of the Worshipful Master I invest you with this jewel to show that you are qualified for Advancement.

Worshipful Master

Your instruction, however, must be postponed as other business presses us. We are about to close our labours by consecrating the edifice to the service of Him in whose name it was erected and we wish to assure ourselves that it is in every respect complete.
(Junior Deacon takes a short step backwards allowing room for Senior Warden to restrain Candidate in what follows)

Worshipful Master

(To Inspector)

Say then, Brother Inspector, if any defect has fallen under observation.

Inspector

(Rising, with sign of Fidelity)

Whilst removing the scaffolds from the building we encountered an obstacle which remains to be overcome. The roof of the vault beneath the Sanctuary, being supported upon the framework which cannot be taken away without endangering its safety, something seems to be needed to secure it.
(Inspector resumes his seat)
(Candidate, urged by Senior Deacon, attempts to step forward and explain)

Candidate

(The only time that the Candidate has been briefed in advance) Oh! But Sir...
(But he is interrupted by Senior Warden)

Senior Warden

(Restrains Candidate with his left arm) Silence!

Narrator

The Senior Warden at this point would normally leave his chair, beckon the Junior Warden to join him, and both would proceed to the Worshipful Master where there would be a long conference in the course of which the Junior Warden would be instructed in the principles of the Arch and its uses as discovered by Hiram Abiff. They would then return to their seats. We have not asked them to enact this part of the ceremony as it would take up too much time. The Worshipful Master continues as from there.

Worshipful Master

This portion of the work was in the hands of our lamented colleague Hiram, reserved to him because of its connection with our mysteries, and this drawing *(exhibits it)* represents a stone which would complete the structure. It was certainly wrought by him and, Brother Overseers, you must have seen it.

Master Overseer

(Rises and faces Worshipful Master with sign of Fidelity) A craftsman recently presented such a stone as his work, which we rejected because he admitted he had found it and that it was not his own work. We deemed it useless.

Worshipful Master

Produce him.

Master Overseer

(Points to Candidate)

There he stands at the left of the Senior Warden by whose orders he was seized and detained for improperly attempting to obtain wages. *(Master Overseer sits)*

Worshipful Master

Craftsman, these are serious allegations. Can you exculpate yourself?

Senior Deacon

(Steps forward with sign of Fidelity)

Worshipful Sir, the treatment which my companion has just received at the hands of your officers has had such an effect upon him that I am compelled to speak for him. My companion, having earned some repute as a skilled craftsman and being anxious to obtain promotion, prepared his own masterpiece and was on his way hither to submit it for your inspection. On his way he observed, half buried in the side of a stream, a stone of curious shape and beauty inscribed with a special monogram. He extracted and cleaned it and while doing so he speculated on its possible uses. It dawned on him that it might be applied to lock stones together and sustaining them in the position of a fully drawn bow. Exchanging this curious stone for his own he hastened here to submit it to the Overseers.

To his dismay they spurned him and his masterpiece and gave him no opportunity to explain his ideas. The stone was thrown away and he himself sternly dismissed with the words 'Go, your conduct is indefensible'.

Making his way to the Senior Warden, to whom he sought to explain himself, he was detained as an impostor. Utterly stupefied he lost heart, but having at last gained your attention, he craves an opportunity to seek for the rejected stone, thus proving his veracity.

Worshipful Master

His request is reasonable. He may search for the stone.

(Senior Deacon resumes his seat. Junior Deacon escorts Candidate round the Lodge while the narrator is speaking)

Narrator

(Waits until Junior Deacon and Candidate are well under way before speaking)

As you see, brethren, the candidate is being led in a somewhat serpentine fashion to represent his descent along a steep and winding path which led from the top of the mountain down to the Valley of Jehosophat, in the floor of which the Brook Kedron flowed.

(Pauses, if necessary, until Junior Deacon and Candidate start back along North side of Lodge)
We have not asked him to return by the same path as, of course, he would have done. We have portrayed him as returning direct to the Master.
(Having made a complete circuit of the Lodge the Junior Deacon leads the Candidate along the North of the lodge and as he passes the secretary's table the Candidate stubs his toe against the stone. The Candidate is instructed to pick up the stone)

Candidate

(Picks up stone and, prompted by Junior Deacon)

I have found it and it is uninjured.
(Junior Deacon & Candidate proceed to Worshipful Master's pedestal where they are joined by Senior Deacon. Candidate in centre, Junior Deacon on his right, Senior Deacon on his left. Candidate hands stone to Worshipful Master)

Worshipful Master

(Having examined the stone)

This is the very stone which no craftsman could be found to make and the characters upon it prove it to be the work of Hiram. The ignorance of the Overseers caused it to be rejected when it is destined for honour.
(Worshipful Master places the stone on his pedestal)

Worshipful Master

(To Candidate)

Upon a subsequent occasion and in a separate ceremony you will be assisted to insert the keystone in its proper place in the Arch, which will finally set the seal upon your achievement. Your are now permitted to retire to restore yourself to your personal comfort.
(Without salute, Junior Deacon, Candidate, & Senior Deacon, in that order, withdraw to the Tyler's room where they remove their working aprons. The Candidate is divested of money and valuables but unknown to him, but clear to those watching, the Senior Deacon will slip a shilling into his pocket. This activity takes place while the narrator is speaking)

Narrator

After adjusting his clothing the candidate is divested of all money and valuables but, unbeknown to him, the Senior Deacon slips a shilling into his pocket.
(Senior Deacon does so).
The Deacons re-enter with him and the candidate is instructed to salute in the Third Degree, penal sign only.
The ceremony resumes from there.

Senior Deacon

(Senior Deacon, Candidate, & Junior Deacon, in that order, re-enter the Lodge)

Salute the Worshipful Master as a Master Mason, penal sign only.

Worshipful Master

Brother Senior Deacon, you will instruct the candidate to advance to the pedestal in the usual manner.
(The Deacons escort the Candidate to a position West of the Central Pedestal and four long paces from it)

Senior Deacon

The method of advancing in this degree is by four gliding or sliding steps, thus. *(Senior Deacon demonstrates)* You will now copy me.
(Candidate does so by slightly bending knees, sliding feet along the ground, starting with the right. Junior Deacon, on the left of the Candidate, does the steps at the same time)
(Worshipful Master gavels, answered by Wardens. All rise. Worshipful Master proceeds to the East side of the pedestal. All give sign of fidelity)

Worshipful Master

You have proved the soundness of your pretension and have established your title to advancement. You must first take an obligation as to the duties and privileges you are about to share. Kneel as a Fellowcraft and place your right hand upon the V.S.L. and say after me:

Candidate

(repeats after the Master)

I {name},
/ In of my own free will and accord /
/ promise to act as a true /
/ and faithful /
/ Mark Master /
/ and to keep my mark unchanged. /
/ I also promise /
/ that I will never unjustly /
/ use any brother's mark /
/ but I will grant his request /
/ if just and within my power /
/ but I shall not feel bound /
/ to relieve him again /
/ until he shall have redeemed his mark /
/ from his former obligation. /
/ Should I be unable to assist him /
/ I will return his mark /
/ together with the cost thereof /
/ which is half a Jewish shekel. /
/ I will also conceal /
/ the Grand Cipher of the Degree /
/ and promise to destroy /
/ the key after using it /
/ and in all respects preserve the secrets /
/ and discharge the duties assigned to me /
/ as I ought to do. /
/ This I swear /
/ on my honour /
/ under the penalty /
/ of having my right ear cut off /
/ my right hand severed at the wrist /
/ and being flung headlong /
/ from the walls of the building /
/ which I shall thereby /
/ render myself unworthy /

/ of working upon. /
/ So help me God /
/ and keep me steadfast in this /
/ my solemn undertaking. /

Worshipful Master

You will now seal this with your lips four times upon the Sacred Volume.
(Candidate does so. All drop sign of fidelity)
(Worshipful Master takes Candidate's right hand with the current Mark Master Mason's pass grip with the thumbs flat and parallel with each other)

Worshipful Master

Rise newly obligated Mark Master.
(Worshipful Master returns to the East. Junior Deacon, Candidate and Senior Deacon, in that order, proceed to the North East for Candidate's 'Trial', as in E.A. Degree)
(At this point there is a loud knock upon the door)

Inner Guard

(With sign of Fidelity)

Brother Junior Warden, there is a report.

Junior Warden

Enquire who wants admission.

Inner Guard

(Opens door)

Wherefore this report?

Tyler

This is an urgent message for the Worshipful Master from a distressed Mark Mason.
(Inner Guard takes the message, plus Mark, in an envelope and closes the door)

Inner Guard

(With sign of Fidelity)

Worshipful Master, there is an urgent message for you from a distressed Mark Mason.

Worshipful Master

Let me se it.
(Inner Guard takes the envelope containing the message and mark to the Master, hands it to him, and awaits an answer)
(Worshipful Master reads the message then hands the envelope, mark and message to the Inner Guard who passes them to the Candidate. Inner Guard remains standing)

Worshipful Master

You will read the letter aloud.
(It is advisable, in a large room, for the Candidate to turn towards the West while reading out the letter so that all can hear)

Candidate

(Reads)

'Dear Brother, I am in great distress and the loan of a small sum of money would assist me. Please lay my claim before your latest obligated member. The only security I have to offer is my mark which is to be retained until the money is repaid.'
(Candidate returns letter and envelope to Inner Guard without comment, but retains the mark)

Worshipful Master

Well, are you going to help him?

Candidate

(Prompted by Senior Deacon)

I cannot as I have no money.

Worshipful Master

Then you must return his mark.
(Candidate hands the mark to the Inner Guard, who remains standing)

Worshipful Master

Do you return the mark and thereby violate the obligation you have so recently sworn to observe? Remember that you are pledged to receive a brother Mark Master's request or at least to return his mark with an amount of half a shekel. Where is the equivalent you have sworn to return with the mark to its owner?

Candidate

(Prompted by Senior Deacon)

I have nothing on my person whatsoever.

Worshipful Master

Perhaps you have not examined your pockets sufficiently carefully. You will please do so now.
(Candidate does so and, with obvious astonishment, finds the shilling. Senior Deacon takes Candidate to the pedestal where Candidate hands the shilling to the Master)

Worshipful Master

As at your Initiation into Masonry this test was designed to teach a lesson, namely, that you cannot be too careful in investigating every factor which may bear upon any problem, not only of other men's conduct but also of your own. Having already chosen a mark as a Mark Mason I now direct you to attend at the Registrar's table where you will sign your name in the lodge book so that none other may use your mark so long as you live.
(Worshipful Master hands shilling to Inner Guard)
(Senior Deacon leads Candidate to the secretary's table, Junior Deacon follows and stands on left of Candidate. Inner Guard returns to his place, via the South side of the lodge, with the envelope, message, mark and shilling)
(Candidate signs the book and is given a drawing of his mark in exchange)

Registrar

You will take this drawing of your mark to the Junior Warden.
(Senior Deacon leads Candidate to Junior Warden's pedestal, Junior Deacon follows and stands on left of Candidate. Candidate shows mark to Junior Warden who inspects it)

Junior Warden

Your mark will distinguish all work done by you or under your supervision. You must preserve it carefully as it cannot be changed without the consent of the lodge. Pass to the Senior Warden with this certificate.
(Junior Warden folds the paper in two and hands it to the Candidate who puts his mark in his pocket. Senior Deacon conducts Candidate to a position to the South of the Senior Warden's pedestal and four long paces from it. Junior Deacon follows and stands on left of Candidate)

Senior Deacon
(With sign of Fidelity)

Brother Senior Warden, I present Brother [name] to receive his wages.

Senior Deacon
(To Candidate)

Advance as a Mark Master to receive your wages. Take four gliding steps as before.
(Deacons and Candidate take four gliding steps starting with the right. They arrive in front of the Senior Warden's pedestal and turn West to face him)

Senior Warden

Your discovery and its successful application not only entitle you to your wages *(Senior Warden gives Candidate a coin)* which I now pay you but also to a knowledge of the Grand Cipher of the Degree.
(Senior Warden displays a card on which are the appropriate symbols to enable the 'Lattice' form to convey letters)
Provided that the key is known this enables brethren to convey messages to each other without the understanding of others.
From this is derived the Grand Sign of the Degree.

The Senior Deacon will now lead you to the Worshipful Master.
(Junior Deacon resumes his seat)
(Note: Throughout the next section the rubric 'demonstrates' implies that the Master demonstrates the action and the candidate copies him)

Worshipful Master

(Stands)

I now entrust you with the other secrets of the Degree. Place your hands on your hips, thumbs pointing backwards *(demonstrates)*, throw back your head as if looking up at a height *(demonstrates)*, and then bring your right hand upwards and outwards thus *(demonstrates)*. This alludes to the method in which unwanted material was heaved over the walls.

The grip or token is given as in the Entered Apprentice's Degree save that in this case you will insert the paper on which you have written your mark between your thumb and the Brother's knuckles *(demonstrates)*. This grip demands a word which is *amasson* and denotes strength or power.

There is another sign with which you must be familiar because it is the method by which you apply for your wages at the Senior Warden's pedestal. With the first and second fingers of your right hand extended and the third and fourth fingers closed into the palm *(demonstrates)* you place your mark across the extended fingers *(demonstrates)* and in this position slide your hand along the top of the pedestal towards the Senior Warden. He will then place your wages upon the mark and you will close the thumb over it and in this position slowly withdraw your hand.

And, finally, the Penal Sign. This is given with the fingers of your right hand held as when receiving wages. You then raise the hand so that the extended fingers are behind your right ear, then drop the right hand in front of you and strike the right wrist with the edge of the left hand *(demonstrates)*. This is in allusion to the penalty of your obligation of having your right ear cut off and your right hand severed at the wrist.

I now invest you with the jewel of the Degree *(pins it to the left breast)*. It is intended not only to show you that you have been accepted into this honourable Degree but also to remind you of the fallibility of human judgement and of your own liability to err. It is also a warning against hasty conclusions as to the character and behaviour of others and is a token of humility. The letters on the jewel are H T W S S T K S and are understood to mean: 'Hiram The Widow's Son Sent To King Solomon'.

I now invite our Brother Inspector to explain to you the working tools of a Mark Master Mason.

Inspector

(Rises and faces Candidate)

They are the Chisel and Mallet.
The Chisel morally demonstrates the advantages of discipline and education. The mind, like the diamond in its original state, is rude and unpolished: but as the effect of the chisel on the external coat soon presents to view the latent beauties of the diamond, so education discovers the latent virtues of the mind, and draws them forth to range the large field of matter and space, to display the summit of human knowledge, our duty to God and man.

The Mallet morally teaches to correct irregularities and reduce man to a proper level, so that by quiet deportment he may, in the school of discipline, learn to be content. What the mallet is to the workmen, enlightened reason is to the passions: it curbs ambition, it depresses envy, it moderates anger and encourages good dispositions – whence arises among good Masons that comely order:

'Which nothing earthly gives, or can destroy,
The soul's calm sunshine, and the heartfelt joy.'

(Inspector sits. Candidate faces the Master)

Worshipful Master

Finally, I congratulate you on being thought worthy to be promoted to the honourable Degree of Mark Master Mason.
While such is your conduct as a Mark Master, should misfortune assail you, your friends forsake you, malice persecute you and evil traduce your good name, ever remember that among Mark Masters you will find those who will administer relief to your distress and comfort in your affliction, and ever bear in mind as an encouragement to hope for better prospects under all kind of fortune that the Stone rejected by the Overseers, possessing virtues to them unknown became, not only the Head of the Corner, but also the Keystone of the Arch.

(The Senior Deacon leads the Candidate to a seat on his right. Both sit)

Before Closing

Worshipful Master

(Gavels Once)

Brother Senior Warden, are the dues all rendered and the wages paid?

Senior Warden

(With sign of Fidelity)

The dues are all rendered and the awards are ready for payment.

Worshipful Master

Brother Junior Warden, you will assist your Brother Senior Warden in their distribution. Brother Deacons, you will arrange the Brethren in the North.
(Junior Warden takes station at the right of the Senior Warden, with the axe in his hands)
(The Brethren will form a procession in the North, then led by the Senior Deacon, they will pass round the Lodge singing the Mark Master's song, first and third verses only. On arrival at the Senior Warden's pedestal each will slide his right hand along the top of the pedestal and will receive their wages from the Senior Warden. Each brother will then return directly to his seat in the lodge. The Candidate, who will be the last in the procession, will be conducted, by the Junior Deacon, to his seat on the right of the Senior Deacon. The Junior Deacon will then resume his own seat)

Senior Warden

(With sign of Fidelity)

Worshipful Master, the dues are all rendered and the wages paid.

Closing

Worshipful Master

(Gavels)

Brethren, assist me to close this Mark Masters Lodge.
Brother Junior Warden, what is the constant care of every Mark Master Mason?

Junior Warden

(With Penal sign of a Mark Master Mason)

To prove the Lodge close tyled.

Worshipful Master

Direct that duty to be done.

Junior Warden

Brother Inner Guard, prove the Lodge close tyled.
(Inner Guard knocks, Tyler knocks)

Inner Guard

(With Penal sign)

Brother Junior Warden, the Lodge is close tyled.
(Junior Warden Knocks)

Junior Warden

(With Penal sign)

Worshipful Master, the Lodge is close tyled.

Worshipful Master

Brother Senior Warden, the next care?

Senior Warden

(With Penal sign)

To see that the Brethren appear to order as Mark Masters.

Worshipful Master

To order, Brethren, as Mark Master Masons.
(All stand to order, hands on hips with thumbs pointing backwards)

Worshipful Master

Brother Senior Warden, your place in the Lodge?

Senior Warden

In the West.

Worshipful Master

Your duty?

Senior Warden

As the Sun sets in the West to close the day so the Senior Warden is placed in the West to close the Lodge, at your command, after having paid the wages if any be due.

Worshipful Master

Brethren, as every degree has a tendency to inculcate the principles of pure morality it is invariably a duty incumbent upon us to countenance and encourage it to the utmost of our power and while we continue faithfully to discharge the duties of that important trust, may the favour of Heaven rest upon us and all regular Masons, to unite and cement us together in the bonds of Friendship and Brotherly love.

(*All*)

So mote it be.

Worshipful Master

Brother Senior Warden, the labours of this Degree being ended you have my command to close this Mark Master Masons Lodge.
(Worshipful Master Gavels with his right hand and does not resume sign)

Senior Warden

Brethren, in the name of the Grand Omnipotent, and by command of our Worshipful Master, I close this Mark Master Masons Lodge.
(All drop sign)
(Senior Warden Gavels repeated by Junior Warden, Inner Guard and Tyler)
(Junior Deacon adjusts Tracing Board to First Degree. Preceptor adjusts square and compasses likewise)
(All team sit)

Narrator

Brethren, this ends the demonstration of the Mark Mason and Mark Master Mason degree ceremonies. In older practice the Worshipful Master would then close the Craft Lodge in the three degrees.
In order to save time the Lodge will be assumed closed in the Third and Second Degrees.
I therefore invite the Worshipful Master to close the Lodge in the First Degree or declare it closed, according to his pleasure.

Worshipful Master

(Worshipful Master rises. All stand)
In the name of the G A O T U, I declare this Lodge closed in the First Degree.
(Gavels)
(Junior Deacon closes Tracing Board. Preceptor closes V.S.L. and extinguishes the candles on the pillars in the centre of the Lodge)

Worshipful Master

Brethren, the first verse of the National Anthem will now be sung.
(The Provincial Grand Master, if present, the Worshipful Master of the demonstration and any other Senior Officers withdraw from the Temple).